5 WHEELS TO SUCCESSFUL SIGHT-SINGING

John Bertalot

Augsburg Fortress • Minneapolis

Cover illustration: Joan Goldsborough
Cover design: Lecy Design

Library of Congress Cataloging-in-Publishing Data

Bertalot, John.
    Five wheels to successful sight-singing: a practical approach to teach children (and adults) to read music/ John Bertalot.
        p. cm.
    ISBN 0-8066-2692-5
    1. Sight-singing. 2. Choral singing—Instruction and study.
I. Title. II. Title: 5 wheels to successful sight-singing.
MT870.B489F6   1993
782.5'1423—dc20   93–2008
                                                            CIP
                                                            MN

The paper used in this publication meets the minimum requirements of American National Standard for Information Sciences—Permanence of Paper for Printed Library Materials, ANSI Z329.48–1984   ∞™

Manufactured in the U.S.A.   AF 11–26925

97   96   95   94   93   1   2   3   4   5   6   7   8   9   10

Dedication

This book is dedicated to:
The Organ Scholars and Assistant Organists of Trinity Church,
Princeton, New Jersey, 1983–1992,
with whom it has been both an education and delight to work,
especially
Elisabeth Caruso Gray
Chris Titko
Ken Lovett
Anne Smith Timpane
Kevin McClure
Eric Plutz
Rodney Ayers
and Greg Vick
and upon whom I modeled the student in this book.

A special dedication to Brian, Chris, Luke, and Matt, the four boys
in Chapter 10 who reformed almost instantly, as narrated,
and became strong mainstays in my boys' choir.

And in loving memory of Irene Willis
my first Associate Director of Music at Trinity whose idea it was
that this book be written, and whose life was tragically cut short by
cancer twelve months after she was appointed Director of Music of
St. James' Church, Madison Avenue, New York City.

Contents

Preface

ONE AFTERNOON I was rehearsing our girls' choir at Trinity Church in Princeton; we were singing a chorus from Duruflé's *Requiem*. The girls were marvelous. Their tone was exquisite, their expression was sensitive, the notes were right, and the atmosphere was thrilling. Halfway through one of the choruses Irene Willis, my associate, walked in and stood there quietly, listening.

When we had finished she said, "Beautiful! How long have you been rehearsing that?"

"The girls were sight-singing it," I answered with considerable pride. "They've never seen it before."

"There can't be many choirs who can do that, can there?" she enthused. (Irene was a great one for handing out compliments.) "Why aren't there more of them?"

"I've no idea," I replied. "It all seems so obvious to me and to the girls."

"You ought to write a book," she replied, "to tell us how you do it."

So I did!

I am grateful to Elisabeth Caruso Gray, to Trinity choirparent Sarah Antin, and to Trinity's new associate organist Nancianne Parrella for their many practical suggestions in helping me prepare this book.   J.B.

1

The Beginning

O NCE UPON A TIME, there was a music student who longed to become a successful choir director, especially of children's choirs. As a child, he sang in a local church choir and grew to love the weekly practices with his friends. The choir was conducted by a kindly woman who loved her choir, loved her music, and loved her church. She was not particularly skilled at choir training, but her care for everyone who was involved with the choir program helped to make every practice and service special. The student longed to train a choir like she did, but to do it better, much better.

When he graduated from high school, he enrolled as a student in music college where he was sure he would learn everything he needed to know about choir training. But it didn't work out like that. The student learned how to play Bach and Messiaen very well and enjoyed many fascinating lectures from inspiring professors, but he was not taught how to train children who knew no music.[1]

"This is what I need to know," he thought, "for this is the situation I shall be faced with when I graduate and go out into the real world!"

He sang in the college choral society and was thrilled when

---

[1] Westminster Choir College in Princeton, New Jersey, does offer such a course to its students. It was begun in the mid-1980s by Irene Willis, Frauke Haasemann, James Litton, and John Bertalot.

the time came for concerts in the city when singers were accompanied by skilled orchestras and led by inspiring conductors. He learned much about the history of music and how to produce his voice, but he had no idea what he would do when he was faced with a choir of his own, few of whom would be trained singers. "What would I say to them at my first practice?" he wondered. "I have no idea how to organize a choir program or how to motivate children to want to turn out to a choir practice on a wet Monday night!"

To see what he could learn, he visited church choirs in nearby towns that had children's programs. He learned a great deal, especially what not to do!

He attended one choir practice where the choir director had difficulty controlling the children.[2] They paid little or no attention to what he was saying. In fact, the children, not the choir director, controlled the practice. Most of the children looked bored and only one or two of the older girls did any singing. "I don't want a choir like that," the student thought.

He visited another church[3] where the choir director was energetic and inspiring. The well-lit practice room had brightly colored pictures on the walls. Neatly arranged on tables were glockenspiels and drums that the children played from time to time.

He enjoyed watching the practice, but realized after it was all over that the children hadn't really done much singing. When they did sing, the songs were musically unremarkable and pitched low, around middle C.

"They had lots of fun," he said to himself as he rode on the bus back to college, "but they seemed to be more of a music club, playing all those instruments. I think the sort of choir I'm aiming for wouldn't have time to play bells and bang drums—except at Christmas!"

As he got off the bus he thought, "I want a choir of children who can sing some of the world's finest music and who really enjoy the challenge and thrill this can provide."

He opened the door to his room and looked at copies of some choral works he had collected. They were by Bach, Handel,

---

[2] This refers to the author in his early days, not to any choirmaster known to him at the present time.
[3] Drawn from observing many choirs elsewhere in the United States.

Palestrina, Britten, Poulenc, Bruckner, and by many modern American composers, such as Gerald Near and William Albright. "Most children wouldn't know where to begin if I handed them one of those," he thought. "Some have difficulty singing even a simple song accurately. I want to discover how I can do better than that!"

In order to try it for himself, the student went to his dean of students to ask if he could take a part-time job as organist and choirmaster of a local church.

"Yes, of course," said the dean, "I have the very place for you. There is a church on the other side of town with a choir of eight children and ten adults who rehearse once a week. There is one service on Sunday and the organ isn't bad, either," he added.

He was interviewed by the minister and was hired. He would start the next week.

"Now I can really begin," he thought with some excitement. "I'll show them just how thrilling it can be to belong to a fine choir!"

But his first practice was a disaster. Only six of the children showed up, and three of them were late. He found that they didn't really show much interest in singing and paid little attention to what he tried to teach them. He was glad that their practice lasted only half an hour, but he felt sure that the practice with the adults would be much better.

It wasn't. Although the adults received him kindly for the most part, the tenor clearly didn't like him and only sang when he felt like it. Several of the altos sang flat and one of the basses couldn't pitch notes accurately. One of the sopranos had a terrible vibrato. All in all, they made a nasty noise.

"They're not a choir," he thought to himself as he wrestled with a simple anthem they seemed to be re-composing afresh every time they sang it. "They're a collection of singers who don't blend, don't sing together, don't read music, don't sing in tune, and have even less idea of what it's all about than I have."

The children were more subdued in the presence of the adults, but they hardly sang anything. They didn't look at the music and tended to play around when they thought he wasn't looking and sometimes when they knew he was!

That was the longest ninety minutes the student had ever

spent, and he was mightily relieved when the practice was over. "Is this really what I want to do with the rest of my life?" he asked himself as he walked back to the college in the rain. "There must be answers somewhere if I only knew where to look."

During the next few weeks, some things improved, but others got worse. Three children quit, but one new one joined. The new boy couldn't match pitch but for some reason he was very interested in the choir and sang all the time, very inaccurately. The student found that he dreaded the children's practice because he didn't know how to go about making them want to learn to sing three hymns every week.

"I don't think I'd be very interested in spending time in a cold church once a week," he thought during one of his walks back to college, "if I knew that I had only hymns to sing, and that I had to learn them by rote, line by line. That's boring!"

He found that he couldn't really keep order. The boys and girls spent much of their time playing around. They hardly ever really listened to what he was saying. One girl in particular was consistently inattentive. He had to keep correcting her. She did what he said for a minute or so, and then relapsed so he had to speak to her again. "She doesn't like me at all," he thought, "and I feel the same way about her!" He decided to leave the church at the end of the semester.

The adults did improve. Surprisingly, the tenor invited him for a meal one evening. The student discovered that the man was quite an interesting person. He'd sung in several good choirs when he was younger and missed the challenge of rehearsing worthwhile music.

"I've rather lost heart," he said to the student. "We sing the same half-dozen anthems over and over, and there's no challenge in anything we do."

That gave the student an idea. He went to the minister to ask if the choir could sing a special anthem on his last Sunday.

"Yes, of course," said the minister, "but I'm sorry you will be leaving us. You are just beginning to make a difference here. However, I really think you need to work with an experienced choirmaster to learn firsthand how to handle a choir. I believe you have it in you to become a good choirmaster." The minister stood up and said, with a twinkle in his eye, "You might not think at the moment that you can do it, but I am sure you can."

These pastoral words cheered the student enormously and he almost wanted to withdraw his resignation, but he knew that the minister was right. He needed to learn by watching someone who really knew how to do the job, but where would he find such a person?

He almost enjoyed his last few weeks at the church. The choir rose to the challenge of the new anthem and the children began to perk up a bit, too. Two new adults joined the choir for the weeks leading up to the last service of the season. He was almost sorry when the time came to say goodbye.

The girl he often had to correct even sent him a thank-you card that she'd drawn herself. He kept that card for a long time. He wondered why it was she who had sent it, instead of one of the other children who had tried harder. "Perhaps I'll know one day," he said to a fellow student as they packed for the vacation. "I only wish I knew what to do now. I really want to become a proficient choirmaster, but I just don't know how to go about it. My organ playing is improving week by week, but that's not all I'm looking for."

"I've heard that the position of assistant organist at a large church in the city has become vacant," said his friend. "Why don't you apply for it? They have over 100 singers in their choirs. The place is swarming with children and adults, and the choirmaster really knows his stuff. There's a superb organ there, too," he added. The student applied for the position and was hired. It completely changed his life.

2

The Turning Point

The choirmaster of the church was a jolly man. His eyes twinkled when he talked and he seemed to have a lot of energy. "Well now, young man," he said as he sat the student down in his untidy office, "what do you want to gain from being my assistant?" He looked the student directly in the eye and waited for his answer.

"Well, sir," he answered, "I want to learn how to become a fine choirmaster. I've tried my hand at it, but nothing really seemed to work. I don't know where to begin."

"I've spent my entire life in church music," answered the choirmaster. "I've made many mistakes. I've learned a lot wherever I've been and I'm still learning."

"I'd love to know what you know," said the student wistfully. "I've looked everywhere for answers, but haven't found them."

"You'll find them here, young man," said the choirmaster encouragingly, "if you keep your eyes and ears open. There's no time like the present," he said as he stood up. "Come and watch me lead a rehearsal with some of my children; they're mostly fifth graders. We start in ten minutes."

"What are you rehearsing with them?" asked the student, as he followed the choirmaster out of his office.

"We've rather a lot on at the moment," answered the choirmaster as he led the way down the stairs to the practice room. "We have a couple of big services coming up this month, so we'll run through half a dozen anthems and also look at some new music for a concert we're giving next month."

"You must spend a lot of time teaching notes," commented the student conversationally. "How do you find time to do that?"

"I find time precisely because I don't teach notes," said the choirmaster. He stopped in his tracks and looked at the student very intensely. "We sing so much music here, sometimes three anthems a week, sometimes more, that everyone has to be able to read the music I give them, and do it well the first time with the minimum of help from me."

"How on earth do you do that?" asked the student, as he tried to get a more comfortable position on the stairs.

"There are two great secrets in the art of training a choir that very few people know," answered the choirmaster. "On these two great secrets hang all my so-called choir training technique."

"Did you learn the great secrets at college?" asked the student.

"No!" said the choirmaster as he turned to lead the way down the remaining stairs, "I learned them from watching other people, from keeping my eyes and ears open, and through trial and error. I've never seen them written in any book on choir training and very few of my colleagues seem to know about them. Yet, I believe they are absolutely central if you really want to bring out the best from both children and adults. I often wonder how I managed to get through so much of my professional life without knowing what I know now!" the choirmaster added with a wry laugh.

"Even if we didn't have to sing all that music every week, I'd still teach them to sight-sing because it's a skill that will remain with them for the rest of their lives. It's so simple to do, if you know how."

"What are these two great secrets?" asked the student eagerly, for he now knew that he had come to the right place and the right person to learn what he really wanted to know. "You obviously feel very strongly about them," he added.

"I won't tell you now," said the choirmaster as he led the way into the practice room. "You can discover them for yourself, for I'll demonstrate them both to you during the next ninety minutes; then we can talk."

The student sat behind a choir bench in the corner of the practice room and watched what the choirmaster did. It was a revelation. He'd never seen anyone lead a rehearsal quite like that. The eight children were punctual. Two even came fifteen minutes early. All were lively and very attentive. They all worked solidly for an hour, with only a couple of moments for relaxation. The pace was fast, the standard of concentration was of a quality that the student had never experienced, except in the college chamber choir. "In some ways, these children are better than some college students," he thought. "They can all read music. How does he do it?"

3

A Practical Secret

A FTER THE REHEARSAL WAS OVER and the last two children were leaving, the choirmaster called the student over to talk. "Have you discovered the two great secrets?" he asked.

"I don't think so," answered the student, who was in something of a daze at all he had seen and heard.

The choirmaster looked directly at the student and said, "We will deal with only one of them now, even though you have seen enough in the last ninety minutes to discover what they both are. Let me ask you the right questions so you can give me the right answers. Tell me what happened at the beginning of the practice," the director asked. "What did we do after the warm-ups?"

"Well," answered the student slowly, so that he could have time to think, "you rehearsed a couple of hymns."

"Yes, I did. How did I introduce them?"

"You told the children the number of each hymn and then they sang a couple of verses," answered the student, rather uncertain of his ground.

"Yes, but what exactly did I do to get them singing?" persisted the choirmaster.

"Well, you played the tune through for them and then they sang," responded the student somewhat desperately. He really couldn't remember what the choirmaster had done, having been so impressed by the standard of singing of the children.

"No, that's exactly what I didn't do!" said the choirmaster rather strongly.

"Oh, oh," thought the student. "I've got to try harder. This man means business!"

"Look, let's pretend that you are the choir. We'll go through, step by step, exactly what I did. Get a hymnal. Now then," he said when the student was ready, "let's begin.

"Hymn 460!" the choirmaster commanded clearly.

"Sorry," said the student, "I was still trying to think of the right answer to your previous question. What was the number again?"

There was a long silence. The choirmaster asked, "How many times did I tell the choir the number of the hymn?"

"Oh, only once," answered the student.

"Yes, only once! Why?"

"To make sure that they listened to you?"

"Yes. Choir directors have to repeat instructions because the choirs have trained their directors! They have conditioned the director to accept their own low level of concentration so that everything must be said two or three times to enable everyone to hear and respond. I am in charge of this choir and they do things in my way, not vice versa. They know I give an instruction only once and so the choir listens; thus their level of concentration is higher than many singers in many other choirs I know."

"May I write that down?" asked the student searching his pockets for a pencil and paper. "That's the great secret!"

"Yes, you may write it down, but it's not the great secret. Many directors don't know it or, if they do know it, don't put into practice. The great secret is more important than that, but we'll come to it in a moment."

"How do you get a choir that is not used to responding immediately to listen to you when you first tell them something only once?"

"You first of all get their attention. You may have to do this in the old way, by repeating your call for silence. Then you tell them that from now on, when you tell them something you will do it only once. Why do I have this expectation?"

"You do it so they will pay more attention and will gradually improve their standard of singing!" responded the student smiling.

"Precisely!" beamed the choirmaster. "You're beginning to learn."

The student wrote down the choirmaster's secret.

A Practical Secret
Condition choirs so that you have to
tell them only once.

4

The Great Secret

"Now we come to the great secret," said the choirmaster. "What happened when the children located the hymn?"

The student thought furiously. "You played the first note for them and then they sang the first verse."

"That's a little better, but you have still missed the whole point of what I was doing. Look," he said more kindly, "we'll go on imagining that you are the choir and that you've located the hymn. What did I say to them?"

"Sing the first note," answered the student, as he began to understand what the choirmaster had been doing.

"Yes! Absolutely right. What didn't I do?"

"You didn't play the first note for them. They had to imagine it for themselves. Why did you do that? Surely, it would be much quicker to have played the note for them than to spend a few valuable seconds asking for a note that they might have sung wrong."

"Yes, it would have been quicker, but it wouldn't have been better!" answered the choirmaster. "That's where so many choir directors go wrong. They think that the short-term, quick solution is the best. I'm not working for the short-term, I'm working for the long-term. I'm working so that my children, by the time they've been in my choir for three years, can pick up a copy of Handel's *Messiah* and sing any chorus almost right at first sight. Think what a time-saver that is!

"So, why do you think I asked them to sing the note, rather than listen to me play it for them?" the choirmaster asked. "What did they have to look at in order to make an attempt at singing the first note?"

"They had to look at the music!" responded the student eagerly.

"Yes! They had to look at the music intelligently, understanding what it meant. That comes from careful teaching on my part. Use every means possible to get singers to look at the notes intelligently. It will be time very well spent. It repays enormous dividends. By the way," he added, "did it matter if they sang the note right or wrong?"

"I suppose it would be better to have gotten it right."

"Yes, but even if they were wrong, it meant that they had to think. Most choir directors do all the thinking for their singers and their singers will let them! Stimulate the singers to think creatively at all times."

"So, are those the two great secrets?" asked the student.

"No," answered the choirmaster, "but they are secrets that you need to know and put into practice."

"Let me write them down," said the student.

- ***Use every means to get singers to look at the notes intelligently.***
- ***Stimulate the singers to think creatively at all times.***

"Now I really feel that we are about to get to the great secret," smiled the choirmaster. "What did I do after the children had attempted to sing the first note?"

"You played the first note for them and they were pretty close."

"Yes, what else?"

"You told them to sing the first verse," responded the student.

"You are nearly right. I played the first note, and then I played the first chord. Why?"

There was a silence. The choirmaster continued. "Not many choir directors realize that just giving a note is not helpful. Singers need to hear the tonality in which they are singing. The key needs to be established in their minds before they start singing. For example, playing a G and then playing the chord of E flat major gives an entirely different message from playing G and then the chord of C major. Thus, the children are ready to sing the first verse of the hymn.

"What did I not do?" asked the choirmaster.

"You didn't play the tune for them. They had to look at the notes and work it out for themselves," answered the student triumphantly.

"Yes! But of course, this comes only after they've been working with me for a few weeks. How did I structure the rest of the practice?" asked the choirmaster.

"You did exactly the same for every piece of music. First, you told them only once what the next piece was, and they found it quickly. Second, you asked them to sing the first note. Third, you then played the first note and the first chord. Fourth, you told them to start singing without having played the tune to them at all. And fifth, I noticed that you used very little accompaniment once they did start to sing. You didn't help them much!"

"Right, young man!" said the choirmaster, glowing. "I can see that we're going to get on very well. The great secret is that the whole of my practice was geared to sight-singing.

"You see," he went on, "it's no use at all teaching children to sight-sing if you aren't going to allow them to exercise their skills so that they may get better and better with each practice. Some fairly enlightened choir directors practice sight-singing for five minutes. That's no good! They have to practice sight-singing all the time. That way the children have to think for themselves. They really get involved with what they are doing. Children don't go to sleep during my practices," said the choirmaster firmly.

"I really believe I'm beginning to see how to succeed in choir training," said the student. "The children must do the thinking. They are doing the singing and not the choirmaster."

The student wrote down the great secret.

The Great Secret
**Every moment of all practices
must be geared to sight-singing.**

5

The Great Secret Applied

The next day, the student was again sitting in the choirmaster's untidy office talking about all he had seen and heard the previous evening. "I hardly slept at all last night. I was so wound up by everything that happened yesterday. It was so thrilling!"

"Yes, I often feel like that, too," answered the choirmaster. "To do this job well, you have to give yourself wholly to it at all times. When things go well, I share the children's excitement, and when they go badly, I feel I want to give up!"

"Do things sometimes go badly for you?" asked the student incredulously.

"Oh, yes! You can't win all the time; but over a period of months and years, you build up a structure of support from everyone who is involved with the choir. This comes not only through the singers but also their families. It is this structure that holds you up when things seem to go wrong. I spend so much energy encouraging others that when bad moments come, members and their families encourage me."

"I imagine that they feel good about that," commented the student.

"You are very perceptive, young man! Yes, they do. One must allow oneself to be vulnerable, to be fully human, and to admit to mistakes. That way the structure is strengthened. It bends with the wind and doesn't break when a storm comes.

"But let's talk more about the great secret you saw in action yesterday," the choirmaster continued. "So many choir directors don't seem to get the message about gearing the whole of their practices to sight-singing. To me, enabling children to read music is one of the most precious and lasting gifts you can offer them. Without it, they are musically blind. They have to rely on the people next to them to lead them through a piece of music. Many singers stay like that right through adulthood. You do not, as some people seem to think, learn how to sight-sing just through belonging to a good choir.

"For example, recently I met an attorney who was, some years ago, head boy of what is considered to be one of the finest choirs of men and boys in this country. That boy sang the most ambitious church music almost every day for four years. When I met him, he told me that he'd recently joined his local church choir when they sang the "Hallelujah Chorus" from the *Messiah.* He told me he found himself singing the treble part an octave lower because he couldn't read music. You could have knocked me down with a feather.

"There was an intelligent man who had been exposed to all that is best in church music, and yet he is musically blind. It's tragic. There are so many folk like that, not only in this country but also all over the world, who have given three or four of their formative years to singing in children's choirs and yet who come out of it with nothing, except a few happy memories of what fun it used to be. On the other hand, many of my choir children later discover they are leaders in their school and college choirs because they can sing right notes immediately."

"Tell me exactly how you structure your practices to sight-singing," said the student who hadn't been able to get a word in for several minutes.

"You saw precisely how I did it," answered the choirmaster. "Every note, every phrase, and every page the singers have to work out for themselves. Why don't I play the melody line along with them?" he asked suddenly.

"I suppose it is so they will have to think and work it out for themselves."

"Yes, indeed."

"But surely this takes far longer than just playing the note for them on the piano?" responded the student.

"Of course it does," exclaimed the choirmaster, pounding his fist on the desk. "I told you about that yesterday, don't you remember?"

The student, taken aback by this sudden outburst, realized he would have to try harder because he was dealing with a man who had such high standards and strong beliefs. This choirmaster expected his students to remember what they had learned. "Oh, yes, I'm sorry! You said you are working for the long-term good of the children and this takes time."

"That's better," said the choirmaster relaxing back into his chair. "So many choir directors work for the short-term goal of getting the notes right immediately—which means playing them to their kids, which means teaching them by . . . rote! What an awful word that is!" There was a silence.

"Children who are taught only by rote are taught to be wholly dependent on the choir director. When the choir director is there, they can sing the music. When the choir director is not there, they cannot sing the music any more. It's so sad!" he exclaimed, hitting the desk with his fist again. "Those directors have made themselves indispensable to their singers.

"My creed is to make myself dispensable. The children do the singing, I don't. After children have been with me for a year or two, they know all the techniques of choir training that I do. They know them so well I don't have to tell them what to do. I ask them what they should do and, nine times out of ten, they give me the right answer and do it. It's so simple." He got up from his chair and slapped a file cabinet to emphasize his strong feelings.

When he'd settled down again, the student ventured to ask, "So, could you remind me just how you structure practices to sight-singing?"

"Yes," the choirmaster laughed, "you've been very patient. Let's make a concise list:

"1. Play a light accompaniment. Playing loudly, as many choir directors do, doesn't enable the singers to hear themselves. I often play detached so the singers can hear themselves easily in the rests between notes—like this."

"2. Don't play the melody with them—they'll only follow what you do, and therefore give up trying to work out the notes for themselves. So I'd amend what I just did, to this."

"3. When they reach a passage that doesn't go correctly, I ask them if it was right; and if not, what was the problem. They have to do the thinking in my practices.

"4. When the problem has been spotted, I ask for a volunteer to try to sing it correctly. This means that they risk failing in front of their peers, but that's okay. They know I value effort as much as I do accuracy.

"5. If the volunteer doesn't get it right the first time, I ask him or her what the problem was, and give them another try. By the way, they're doing this without me playing the piano for them. They are entirely on their own. If the volunteer doesn't know, I ask for another volunteer. I go round the entire treble line until someone does sing it right. I find that the spirit of competition is so keen in all my children that there's never any shortage of volunteers.

"6. Then I have all the children sing what has just been modeled for them and we go on."

The student was busily writing all these points in his notebook. He looked up when he had finished and commented, "This must give the children a great sense of pride in their achievements."

"Right! They themselves have worked out the right notes for themselves. They have ownership of this music and not me! They will sing it right on Sunday because it's their music, not mine.

That's why we have so many children and adults in our choirs," he added. "Giving ownership of the music to those who will be performing it works for all singers. Do you see now?"

"Yes, I do," said the student. "Thank you."

6

Wheel 1
Passion

"**Y**OU SEE," SAID THE CHOIRMASTER, "what I'm going to give you regarding the teaching of sight-singing can be likened to giving you a brand new car. It has every-thing—a superb engine, gas in the tank, and a key in the ignition. The only thing it doesn't have is wheels and you have to supply those yourself! The first wheel you've already seen."

"Is it the tidy practice room?" asked the student uneasily, fear-ing he might be wrong.

"It could be," said the choirmaster gently. "That certainly helps. But it was something you said to me yesterday about my attitude to this whole situation."

"Oh, yes! I said that you felt strongly about what you are doing."

"That's it!" exclaimed the choirmaster as he slapped his knee and beamed. "But it's even more than that. I feel passionately about what I am doing. You won't achieve anything worthwhile in this life unless you feel passionately about it. A mild sense of good-will or a resolution to reform will do no good. It has to take you over and govern everything you do. Thus, the first wheel is, have a passion for teaching sight-singing!" proclaimed the choirmaster.

"Let me write that down," said the student.

Wheel 1
Have a passion
for teaching sight-singing
and everything else you do.

"This passion shows itself in all sorts of ways," said the choir-master. "It affects your preparation for practices, your punctuality at practices, your pastoral care of the children and adults—every-thing. It ensures that you will spare no effort to ensure that every child who joins your choir will be able to read music in the shortest possible time. It makes life so much easier. When the full choir has to learn a new anthem, all I have to do is to hand it to them and say, 'Sing it!' and they do because they can!

"Children need to be motivated to learn," the choirmaster con-tinued. "They will only learn from you what you really want to teach them. You must believe in the worth of what you are teach-ing. If you really want to teach children to sight-sing, you must have a passion for it.

"How many people do you know who are on perpetual diets?" the choirmaster asked unexpectedly. Not waiting for a response, he continued, "The reason they are on diets is because they are unable to alter their eating habits. Those people who alter their eating habits have no problem with their weight. They have entered into a new mode of living. It's exactly the same with teach-ing children to sight-sing," continued the choirmaster.

"If you will begin to teach the children to sight-sing in the way I shall show you, you must alter the way you lead your choir prac-tices. Leading practices in the old way (when you gave them the right notes to sing and didn't stimulate them to think) will make all your teaching of sight-singing decay. It will not be used in the situa-tion for which it is designed. If you don't use your muscles, they will wither. If you do exercise them, they will grow stronger and ever more useful. So it is with sight-singing.

"I exercise my children and adults in their sight-singing skills throughout every practice so that they get better and better, week by week; and they can see it happening! It's so thrilling. It all comes from having a passion for the task in hand.

"Passion embraces all those points you've already listed. What are they again?"

The student began a fresh page and wrote:

Wheel 1: Passion

- **Preparation for practices**
- **Punctuality at practices**
- **Tell them only once, because you are in charge.**
- **They must look at the notes intelligently**
- **Stimulate the singers to think**
- **Ask them, don't tell them**
- **Allow them to fail**
- **Play light accompaniments**

"Yes, you've listed so many of the things we've talked about, but you've missed many others."

"What are they?" asked the student keenly.

"If you think hard, you'll remember."

"Oh, oh," thought the student, "he's using his choirtraining techniques on me!"

"Come back tomorrow," the choirmaster added as he got up to leave. "Watch me lead a class of four new boys. I'll be starting at the beginning to teach them to sight-sing."

That night the student thought about all they had talked about for those two formative days and tried to remember just what he had missed.

7

Wheel 2
Small Groups

The next afternoon, the student and the choirmaster were standing by the piano in the large, airy practice room. The sun shone through the tall windows and lit up the music stands that were arranged on either side of the piano. Row after row of music boxes neatly lined the walls. Behind the piano was a large chalkboard with a supply of colored chalks.

"This is a marvelous choir room," commented the student.

"Yes, we're very fortunate to have one of the finest practice facilities in this country," answered the choirmaster. "I had these music stands made especially for this room. The children and the adults have to stand for all practices and they love it. They know that we mean business when we come in here. It helps their concentration wonderfully.

"We had the choirmaster of the most famous English men and boys' choir visit us recently. He said he wished he could have such a practice room! When you get your own church, really work to make your practice room comfortable, well-lit with plenty of ventilation, and geared to hard work, and with music filed neatly and readily available," he added. "You see that all singers have their own cubbies with next month's music ready to use. Our librarian is a treasure. I couldn't run the choirs without him.

"It is to this room that singers come week after week from their comfortable homes. Let it be welcoming. Let it be warm in winter and cool in summer. Let it be tidy. Let it be efficient. The importance of having a really good choir room and maintaining it well cannot be over stressed.

"Let's get back to the coming rehearsal. When I was leaving my office yesterday I gave you a hint about the second wheel," said the choirmaster. "How many children did I say were coming to see me this afternoon?"

"Four," answered the student quickly.

"Well done!" exclaimed the choirmaster, smiling. "You listen attentively and so you will do very well here." The student glowed quietly under the choirmaster's approval. "It's almost impossible to teach children to sight-sing really well in a large group. Do you know why?"

"I suppose it's difficult to supervise everyone's progress," ventured the student hesitantly.

"Yes, but it's much more than that. Children are wonderful imitators," explained the choirmaster. "It takes only one child in a group who knows what he or she is doing for everyone else to follow him or her. The others follow so quickly they don't even realize it. They believe they are doing the thinking, when actually, it's someone else. It's even worse than that, for there's someone else who doesn't realize that the children are following a strong leader. Who can that be?"

"The choir director!" responded the student quickly.

"Yes indeed! Some choir directors think all their singers can read music, not realizing that most are following only one or two people in the group who are doing all the leading for the choir. When those one or two are absent, the whole thing collapses. If you have children in small groups, they cannot hide behind anyone else. They have to do all the thinking for themselves!"

"I see," said the student. "The matter of learning to sight-sing is the ability to think creatively—to work out for yourself what the next note sounds like and then sing it."

"My word!" said the choirmaster, "that was very perceptive of you."

The student tried to keep an impassive face, for he had surprised even himself by what he had just said. Perhaps the choirmaster's active thinking had inspired him.

"Write down the second wheel," commanded the choirmaster. The student took out his notebook and wrote:

Wheel 2
Work in small groups.

After the student finished writing, the choirmaster said, "I should tell you that I know one school music teacher who claims that she can teach sight-singing in large groups. She came to some of my practices to see what I was doing. She heard me say that teaching sight-singing doesn't work in big groups. However, two months later she told me she tried my methods and found they did work in the classroom. In fact, she said her most productive singing classes are half-hour sessions twice a week when all the children practice nothing but sight-singing. She told me the children love it.

"But for me," added the choirmaster, "it doesn't work like that. It takes me twice as long to train two children as it does to train one child. It takes twice as long to train four as it does two, and so on. The smaller the group, the more efficient will be your teaching. At least, that's what I've found to be true in my experience."

"Then why are you seeing four children this afternoon instead of just one?" asked the student.

"Because these children want to join the choir now," answered the choirmaster. "There are only so many hours in the day when they can come and when I can fit them in. It doesn't matter if it takes two months instead of one month to teach them how to sight-sing. Their vocal production will be improving all the time. Further, they will be getting a feel of what it's like to become a member of a closely knit team. The extra time will be well spent. If I ask three of them to wait for a month or so until I have taught one child, what are the chances of all three children returning to me?"

"Pretty slim, I should think," responded the student.

"Yes! They will have filled their time with other activities and I'll have lost them. We are in a highly competitive field here," the choirmaster added. "Children have so many demands on their time these days that I have to catch them while they're still willing to be caught!"

"Oh!" exclaimed the student, "I thought you were selective when you audition children for your choirs."

"Good heavens, no!" answered the choirmaster. "I take almost anyone I can get. My job is to turn unpromising children into educated musicians. Where do you think these grey hairs came from?" he asked with a smile, pulling his tangled locks.

"I thought you said that choir training was simple."

"It is," answered the choirmaster. "The road is very clear for those who know where it is, but you have to walk it energetically and full of care for the singers; and that takes a lot out of you. Are you prepared to spend yourself in that way for the rest of your life?"

"I hadn't thought of it like that," answered the student. "When I tried training a choir for six months, it absolutely wore me out with worry."

"That was because you weren't doing it right," said the choirmaster. "Choir training will absolutely wear you out, but the worries will be far outweighed by the rewards and thrills that will come your way at every practice as you watch the children grow in every possible good way. Further, they will love you for it. You are giving them something they can get nowhere else. They know it and their parents know it. What you spend on them, in care and time, you and they will have forever; and that is something money cannot buy."

"Wow!" exclaimed the student. "Let's do it, then."

8

Wheel 3
One Step

"What's the next wheel?" asked the student as he turned a page in his notebook.

"Wheel 3 is obvious—if I ask you the right question."

"I'm listening," responded the student eagerly.

"When you are teaching children, should you teach them skills that they can or cannot achieve?"

"That's easy! You teach them things they can achieve."

"Right! It is vitally important that the children are able to do what you ask them to do. They must succeed in carrying out every challenge you give."

"How do you manage that?"

"You tell me!" said the choirmaster unexpectedly, looking the student squarely in the face.

"Whoops," thought the student, "I was expecting him to do my thinking for me. How easy it is to slip into that mode of not thinking!" There was a silence as the student thought furiously for several seconds, but no answer came to mind.

"Should you teach them in giant leaps or small steps?" the choirmaster asked, breaking the silence.

"Oh, small steps," answered the student gratefully.

"Yes," said the choirmaster. "How many small steps should

you teach at one time?"

"Perhaps two or three," ventured the student, not sure of his ground.

"Try again."

"One or two?"

"You're getting warmer," said the choirmaster patiently.

"One?"

"One indeed! You must realize that you are taking your children on a road they don't know and where they are more likely to be wrong than right. If they are to enjoy this learning experience with you, they need to know they will almost certainly get it right with your help, rather than wrong."

"I see! I know when I've given a right answer to you, I feel good about it."

"Why is that?" inquired the choirmaster.

"People like to be right. It does things to their egos."

"Yes, but there's more to it than that. Who else felt good when you gave a right answer?"

"Well, you did, I suppose," said the student.

"'Suppose' nothing! Didn't you realize that I felt genuine pleasure when you gave me a right answer?" The choirmaster thumped the top of the piano with his fist.

"Oh, yes! You smiled when I got it right. I remember now," said the student, realizing the choirmaster felt strongly about this, too.

"That's better! A choirmaster has to feel genuine pleasure when his children succeed. What else goes with this?"

"The choirmaster has to express that pleasure so that the children know it. It really motivates them to try to succeed because they want to please their director," answered the student.

"Right! How does one ensure a whole stream of right answers?" pressed the choirmaster.

"Teach just one thing at a time so the singer will get it thoroughly right and be successful," answered the student.

"Yes, nothing succeeds like success. Once the children understand that being with you enables them to succeed, then you're on a roll. Write that down."

The student thought for a while, and then wrote:

Wheel 3
Teach one small step at a time.

"You'd be surprised how many choir directors and teachers don't do that," said the choirmaster. "For example, how many things are involved in singing a verse of a hymn correctly?"

The student thought for a while and said, "The notes must be right and so must the words; so I suppose the answer is 'two.'"

"How many things do you have to get right to sing all the notes correctly?"

"The pitch and the rhythm," answered the student, aware he hadn't really been thinking hard enough. "I guess the children must be concentrating on three things to sing a verse of a hymn correctly."

"What about tuning and tone, and breathing and posture, and clear enunciation, and shape of the mouth, and a relaxed jaw, and on and on?"

"Oh," the student sighed. There was a pause.

"Just think how many things are involved in breathing correctly—let alone doing the singing in conjunction with breathing. The list is almost endless."

"I hadn't realized that singing one verse of a hymn involved so many different skills," said the student

"Few choir directors do. That's why many children are not successful in taking these techniques into their innermost being. They are presented with far too many things to think about at one time. They quickly give up and settle for what they can get away with; and their choir directors think that's all their singers can do. They are wrong. Children can achieve far more than most choir directors have ever dreamed!" He thumped the piano again several times.

"That's putting it rather strongly, isn't it?" said the student.

"Maybe it is, but if you don't feel strongly about what you are doing, you won't achieve anything. I feel strongly about it, very strongly, and my children feel strongly, too, otherwise they wouldn't come here!

"Look at Wheel 1 again," said the choirmaster, taking the student's notebook from his hand and turning back several pages. "There, look! Wheel 1: Have a passion for teaching sight-singing and everything else you do."

The student could almost feel the choirmaster vibrating. He certainly had a passion for his work, even if it did lead him to over-state his case—or did it?

9

Wheel 4
Theory and Practice

The sound of children playing outside filtered through an open window. "We must get on," said the choirmaster, "the children will be coming in very soon.

"Wheel 4 is not so obvious, but it is absolutely essential to the success of teaching children sight-singing. I'll get you to tell me what it is," he said, giving the student another of his direct looks.

"He's challenging me again," thought the student. "I need to be on my toes!"

The choirmaster continued, "What's involved in reading music? Or, putting it another way, there are two parts to music; there's the theoretical, and what else?"

"The practical," responded the student.

"And how do they relate to the reading of music?"

There was a pause as the student thought. "The printed page is the theoretical part, and the singing of the notes is the practical."

"Absolutely right!" beamed the choirmaster, showing that he was genuinely pleased with his pupil. "It is vital that whenever you ask the children to sing something, they must also see it written down—even if it's only a single note you are using to help them produce their voices correctly. Let them see their warm-up exercises written on the chalkboard. By the way, always have a chalkboard in your practice room. I can't do without mine. The children must see what they sing," the choirmaster continued. "What follows?"

"They must sing what they see," said the student triumphantly.

"Right! Every theoretical point must be made practical, and made practical immediately. Theory and practice. It's no use spending five minutes learning the names of the notes on the spaces, that's just dry theory. All theory, by definition, is dry, especially for children. What must they do once they know where G is?"

"They have to sing G! Every theoretical point must be made immediately practical," answered the student.

The choirmaster interrupted, "And every practical point must be made theoretical. By the way, what did I do wrong just now in my enthusiasm?" he asked the student.

"You took away from me what I was just about to say," answered the student, hesitantly.

"Yes! I apologize for that. That's something that so many choir directors do, assuming they are enlightened enough to teach through asking questions. Often, they do not allow the child enough time to answer the question fully. You need to watch out for that. It's such an easy trap to fall into," he said with a wry smile.

"Write down the fourth wheel. The more aware you are how closely theory and practice are tied together, the quicker your children will be to learn how to read music."

The student wrote:

Wheel 4
**Every theoretical point must be made practical and vice versa.
"Sing what they see,
See what they sing."**

10

Wheel 5
Steer the Car

The chimes of the church clock striking the hour filled the practice room. "We won't have time to discuss Wheel 5," said the choirmaster. "It's time for the practice to begin."

"There are five wheels?" asked the student. "I thought cars had only four wheels!"

"You've missed the most important one," answered the choirmaster, "but we'll have to go into that another time. It's vital to be punct . . . ." He was unable to finish the sentence. The door burst open and four boys rushed in, talking at the tops of their voices.

The choirmaster sat quietly and watched as the boys approached the piano. The student noticed that the choirmaster had his direct-look expression. He wondered how the choirmaster would deal with the noisy boys.They reminded him of some of the children he had directed. "This I must see," he thought.

The children continued chattering as they gathered around the grand piano. The choirmaster simply folded his arms, leaned on the piano, and looked intently at them.

After fifteen seconds the children noticed that they were being looked at rather directly, and the chattering began to die down. After another few seconds, it stopped entirely and there was silence.

Five more seconds went by. "It seems more like five minutes," thought the student, as the children and choirmaster looked at each other across the piano. "I wonder what he's going to say first? He'll blast them, I know!"

"I'm pleased with you," said the choirmaster, most unexpectedly. "Why am I pleased with you?" One of the boys put up his hand. "Yes, Luke?"

"Because we came in on time," the boy answered.

"Yes! Did we agree last week that being on time would be a good thing to do?"

"Yes, we did," murmured the boys, not quite sure what to make of the situation.

"Yes, we did indeed! What else did we agree on last week—about how the practice should begin?"

There was a pause and another boy spoke, "Because we have all come a long way for practice, we agreed that it would be a good idea if we made the most of our time here."

"Right, Brian! But what does that mean exactly? Yes, Matt?"

"We should come into the room quietly so that we should be ready to start."

"Right again! Were you ready when you came in here, Chris?"

"No, we were talking," answered Chris sheepishly.

"Yes, indeed! Was that helpful, Luke?"

"No."

"Okay. I think you have the message. I'm here to help you become super-singers and we need every moment we have to turn you into practicing musicians. Let's make sure we all know what rules we have agreed upon; and so let's start the practice one more time.

"When I've finished speaking, I want you to go out of the door, wait for ten seconds, and then show me how you really should come into the practice room. Okay? Off you go."

The boys looked at each other sheepishly, but turned round and walked out in a rather surprised silence.

"Wow!" said the student as the door closed behind them, "that was really something!"

"Yes," said the choirmaster, "that's Wheel 5—the steering wheel. The children must learn quickly to respond to what I say.

They must realize that I mean everything I tell them. Children need boundaries within which they can work. If they learn that you don't really mean what you say, they won't know where they are, and they'll call the shots. From the children's very first practice on, they need to know that the boundaries are there to help them achieve the great things that I have in store for them.

"A car that has four fine wheels but no steering wheel is no good. It must go where the driver determines and not vice versa. Children actually prefer order to disorder. I know, because I've asked them, and they've proved it for themselves in practices."

The student wrote in his notebook:

Wheel 5
The driver steers the car, not vice versa.

The door opened and the four boys walked in very quietly and stood around the piano. They looked at the choirmaster and he looked at them. "Am I pleased with you?" he asked.

"Yes," they smiled.

"I'm very pleased with you. Let's begin!" The student knew he was in for a good forty-five minutes, and so did the children.

11

Five Wheels
In Practice

Two days later, after observing a sight-singing session of girls, the student was again in the choirmaster's untidy office. A pile of papers had been cleared from one of the chairs and the student was sitting with pencil and notebook in his hands.

"Well, what did you think of these two sight-singing sessions you observed—the new boys' practice two days ago and the girls' yesterday?" asked the choirmaster leaning back in his chair.

"May I ask you a question first? When the noisy boys came in, why didn't you tell them to be quiet immediately? Isn't that what you wanted?"

"That's a very good question. Let me ask you one. What did I say to the boys as soon as they were quiet enough to hear me?"

"You told them that you were pleased with them because they were punctual."

"Right. You see, I needed to get them into the frame of mind so that they would really hear what I had to say about their noisy behavior. If I had blasted them right away, they would have turned sullen and treated me like an unhelpful taskmaster. Then the practice would have begun badly. That would have set up a negative situation. I had to turn the situation around into a positive one— positive for them and positive for me.

"The easiest way to do that was to say something appreciative, which they knew to be true. That got them listening to me.
Once I had their attention, then I could address the other matter.
By the way," he added, "did I tell them about the noisy behavior or
did they tell me?"

"They told you," the student responded. Then his eyes lit up.
"Oh, I see. When they tell you, they have ownership of the need
to behave well. They wouldn't do it just because you said so, but
they will do it because they said so!"

"Yes, you really are very perceptive, young man. Not many
people would have spotted that, but you did. You have the makings of an alert teacher."

"Let me write down those two helpful hints," said the student
gratefully, opening his notebook:

- *An appreciative remark enables children to*
  hear what you say.
- *Get them to tell you what you really want to*
  tell them. Then they're more likely to do it.

"Much of what we're discussing applies not only to children,"
commented the choirmaster. "It applies equally well to adults. If
you have something difficult to say to an adult, get his or her attention by saying something positive first, then he or she will hear you
more easily.

"Now, tell me what you thought of those two practices," said
the choirmaster.

"Well, you achieved much more with the boys than you did
with the girls," answered the student. "Why was that?"

"You can answer the question yourself," said the choirmaster,
giving him a direct look.

The student thought, "He's challenging me again." After a few
seconds he said, "It was not because the boys were more talented
than the girls or had better voices."

"Right. In fact, some of the girls were more intelligent than the
boys and were much more willing to concentrate for long periods.
It must have been something else. Look at the five wheels again
and tell me which one applies here."

The student thought again for a moment and then exclaimed,
"Of course! It was because you had eight girls and only four boys.
You were able to achieve only half as much with the girls as you

did the boys. It's obvious."

"Everything I tell you is obvious," answered the choirmaster, "at least, it's obvious to me. The trouble is that very few people are able to see the obvious, even when it's right in front of them."

"Does it matter if one group gets on faster than another?" asked the student.

"Not in the least," said the choirmaster. "The important thing is that each group and each child in that group progresses at the pace that is right for them. There are no time constraints here. What matters is that each step in the learning process is covered thoroughly and understood completely by each child. They will all be able to read music within a short time and will get better at it the longer they are in the choir. Why is that?"

"Is it because you keep on encouraging them to sight-sing throughout their choir careers?"

"Yes, but how do I encourage them? We discussed this major point when we first met."

"Oh, yes. You lead every choir practice so that sight-singing is the major focus. You never play the notes for them. The singers have to work them out for themselves. The children do all the thinking in your practices."

"Absolutely right! Learning to sight-sing is a skill that can get better and better. Further, it will remain with them for the rest of their lives—just like reading words on a page."

The student thought a while, "You said that there was a learning process. Could you tell me exactly what that process is?"

"No," said the choirmaster, "it will be much better if . . ." he waited for the student to finish the sentence.

"It will be much better if I tell you what the process is," finished the student. "How do I do that?"

"I'm going to ask you the right questions. The best method of teaching is for the teacher to ask the right question so the students can find the right answer for themselves—they own the answer. You'd better write that down."

The student opened his notebook and wrote:

- ***Teach by asking the right questions.***

12

Step 1
Singing One Note

"L ET'S BEGIN," SAID THE CHOIRMASTER. "There are twelve steps you must take to enable a child, or anyone else for that matter, to be able to read music surely and easily. I've been working at this system all my life and I've proved over and over again that it really works. Other choir directors who have tried it say that it works for them, too." He paused and looked at the student who was waiting to be impressed by the revelation of profound secrets discovered over a lifetime.

"These twelve steps are not difficult or obscure," said the choirmaster, reading the student's thoughts. "They are simplicity itself. Anyone can work out what they are, given a little clear, practical thought." He smiled and said, "Let's begin with you telling me the first step."

The choirmaster leaned forward in his chair, fixed the student with his direct gaze, and asked, "What is the absolute basic minimum skill children have to acquire at the very beginning of their choir careers to enable them to begin to read music?"

After a pause, the student said, "The children must be able to sing the first note correctly."

"Well done! Until a child can pitch one note accurately, there's no point in asking him or her to sing a scale, much less attempt to sight-sing a song. Now, most of the children you heard during the past few days could pitch notes pretty well, but there was one in each group who could not. How did I deal with that situation?"

"You tried several approaches. You asked the boy to try again. If that didn't work, you asked his neighbor to sing the note. I saw that this worked well in one case, but not the other. For the girl with the real problem, who sang under the given note, you changed your note to match the note she sang."

"Yes. A child often finds it hard to pitch a tone from a note played on the piano, but finds it easier when the note is sung by someone else. This is where women choir directors have the advantage over men; they can sing in the right register for children," said the choirmaster.

The student continued, "With the girl, once you agreed on the same pitch, you gradually raised the notes you asked her to sing, going up the scale, one note at a time. That worked for the first two or three notes, but then she got stuck."

"Yes, I had to alter my program quickly for that child. I saw that she couldn't achieve everything I'd originally planned for her. I set a special goal for her. I asked her to sing just those two or three notes correctly, and then left it. Did you notice I showed that I was particularly pleased with what she had achieved during that minute?"

"Yes, I did," responded the student. "She achieved relatively more than the other children because she'd started further back than they had."

"The choirmaster's attitude has to be wholly positive in this process. Children have to realize you are pleased with them because they're trying hard, not because they happen to get things right. A little achievement is all I'm seeking—coupled with total concentration for the whole of the practice. Each child goes at his or her own pace." The choirmaster paused for a moment, and then asked, "Now, why did I spend only a minute with that girl?"

"Because the other children's attention might begin to wander," said the student.

"Yes! It's very important to mix what you are doing with the children. Have them sing briefly by themselves, have them sing in small groups, and then have them sing all together. If you are constantly changing pace, color, and demands, the children will be kept on their mental toes. Have them sing. Have them answer questions. Have them stand. Have them sit. Have them face this way and then that way.

"You noticed how I moved around. I didn't stay sitting at the piano as so many choir directors do. I walked around the children. I had the children stand by me and then stand on the far side of the piano. I asked them to listen to the other children and tell me how they did. At no time was there any doubt that I expected every child to be involved for the whole forty-five minutes. Even when I was dealing with the child who had pitch problems, I involved the other children, too. How did I do that?"

"You asked one of them to sing the note the other child found difficult," answered the student. "You said, 'Who can sing this note for me?' Several of the children put up their hands and you asked one of them to sing it."

"Yes, then I asked the children to raise their hands when the girl sang the note right. That's positive input. She wanted to earn the respect of her peers. All children do, so I enabled this to happen. Then she had her turn at putting up her hand when the other children sang. We were all in it together."

Step 1A: Learning about pulse

The choirmaster paused for a minute. "There's so much to say about choir training techniques, but this is not the time. We can discuss those later. Let's continue with Step 1 in the sight-singing process."

"Singing one note," said the student.

"Singing one note, yes; but there were three other things I did with the children while getting them to sing one note correctly. What were they? By the way, you noticed I asked them to sing middle G for me, not middle C. We'll talk about that later."

"You asked them to sing the note for four counts."

"That's right. It's very important to give the children an exact aim. If they were asked to sing only one note, that would be open ended. When they are asked to sing the note while you count four, they know exactly what they have to do."

The student said, "I noticed that you counted four on your fingers, giving them something to look at. You showed them that they had to stop singing at the count of five when you counted your thumb as five."

"Did you notice if the children got it nearly right or exactly right?" asked the choirmaster.

"Some of them got it exactly right the first time, but others had to give it more than one go," observed the student. "You put one of your five wheels into operation."

"Well done! The children must be able to do what you ask them to do, and you stay with it until they do." The choirmaster got up from his office chair and strode around the room, carefully avoiding a pile of papers on the floor. "I want them to get it right so much that I almost will them to do it right. I know they can and I can picture them doing it right so strongly that they eventually do get it right."

He sat down again, quivering slightly. "That's Wheel 1," he added. "You must have a passion for this business, otherwise it won't work." He smiled at the student who responded with a grin.

Step 1B: Learning about the stave

"The second thing you did in the first practice was to write the note G on the stave on the chalkboard. That was the note you asked them to sing. That was Wheel 4: Every theoretical point must be made practical and vice versa."

"Did I tell them that it was the note G I wrote on the chalkboard?" asked the choirmaster.

"No, you asked them; you didn't tell them. As you began to write the five lines of a stave on the chalkboard, you asked them how many lines it takes to write music. They quickly responded by saying five.

"Then you wrote the treble clef sign on the stave and asked them what that symbol was called. Again, they responded quickly by saying it was a G clef.

"I found it helpful when you asked them, 'Do you know why it's called a G clef? What word is this?' as you wrote 'Good' on the chalkboard, with a scrolled capital G. You explained that the G clef is a sort of old-fashioned G.

"Then you pointed to the circular part of the clef and pointed to the second line up and asked them the name of the note written on that line. With a smile of recognition, the children gleefully responded, 'G.' And you praised them. Then you simply played it for them and they sang it," added the student.

"That's very good," said the choirmaster. "If they hadn't known the answers to those questions, I may have had to tell them, but there's nearly always someone in the group who does know. They are proud to share their knowledge with the other children. You noticed that even when I was writing on the chalkboard, I kept their attention occupied by asking them questions."

"Yes, and every time the children sang that G, you pointed to the note on the chalkboard," said the student. "Sing-See, See-Sing. That's Wheel 4!"

"Well done! Now let's get on to the third part of this first step."

Step 1C: Learning singing techniques

"What was the third thing I taught them while they were singing just one note?"

"Let's see," said the student, consulting his notes. "The first thing you asked them to do was to sustain the note for four counts, coming off on the fifth count as you pointed to your thumb."

"Yes, but did I keep it just to four beats?"

"No, you extended it to five, six, or sometimes up to nine beats, coming off on the tenth. All the while you were counting on your fingers. That helped their breathing technique, which you taught them later. The children really got the message about the length of a note. They had no problem with sustaining long notes for their correct length, unlike many children's choirs I've heard."

"And the second point?" asked the choirmaster

"You taught them the beginnings of written notation, introducing the stave, the clef and the note G. They got that message, too."

"Why did they get the message?"

"Because you taught them one thing at a time—Wheel 3!"

"Right! Now let's get on to the third part. What was that?" asked the choirmaster.

"There were so many things," answered the student. "You taught them how to breathe, how to open their mouths with well-shaped lips, how to stand well—the list seems endless."

"Correct again! The third part was to use the singing on one note to begin to teach them basic singing techniques. Why don't I immediately have them sing complete songs?"

"Because it presents to the children too many things to think about at a time?" responded the student.

"Right! If you want children to succeed—which means getting every point wholly correct—they must attempt only one thing at a time. Learning to breathe, learning to stand well, or learning how to use their mouth and jaw in the correct manner are so much easier if they're thinking of only one note. It's much more fun in the end, too," he continued. "Then they know they are getting it right. They experience the thrill of achievement which is one of the mainstays of my choir.

"These new children get this thrill by singing one note well. The more experienced children are thrilled when they can pick up an unknown anthem and sing it correctly at first sight. The adults are thrilled every week by the standard of polish we can achieve because we don't need to have note-learning sessions. We can spend our time on fine detail. It's all very exciting!"

"Let me write down the first step," said the student, getting out his notebook again.

Step 1: Singing One Note
• learn about pulse
• learn about the stave
• learn singing techniques

"Well, that's enough for today, young man. I'm going to try to get this desk cleared. I think the top is made of wood, but I haven't seen it for several weeks. Come along tomorrow afternoon when two fifth grade girls will be here. They're older than our other new girls, so I'm taking them by themselves. You'll see how quickly they'll pick up these simple techniques."

"That's Wheel 2," thought the student.

"You might like to work out for yourself what the next couple of steps are in the sight-singing process," he added. "They're an extension of Step 1."

"Are they obvious?" asked the student as he opened the door.

"Of course they are! Everything is obvious to me."

"And obvious to the children, too." said the student, smiling.

"When you can teach children in such a way that every new point is obvious to them, then you really will have become a successful teacher!" beamed the choirmaster. "See you tomorrow."

Some helpful hints

The next afternoon the student found a chair and seated himself in the practice room. He had a notebook and pencil in hand ready to take notes on every good thing he saw or heard. He knew he was about to experience another very positive time—both for himself and for the two girls who were coming. He was not disappointed.

The girls arrived promptly and found the choirmaster ready for them. The student observed that the choirmaster had prepared the practice room and was seated at the piano when the girls arrived.

After chatting with the girls for a minute, the choirmaster said, "Okay, let's begin!"

Again, the student thought to himself, "He makes the singers feel welcome by talking with them. But when the time comes to begin the practice, he lets it be known that it is time to start. I should write those two hints down." And so he did:

- *Welcome singers*
- *Be deliberate in beginning practice.*

Opening pattern

The student found that the choirmaster followed Step 1 with the girls, just as he had with the two other groups:

- *Sing one note on a G*
- *Work on the shape of the mouth*
- *Work on breathing and stance*
- *Write on the chalkboard:*
     a stave, a G clef, and the note G
- *Point to the note while the children sing it for four or more beats*
- *Count on fingers to show them exactly when they should come off.*

Model question

The choirmaster never told the singers anything. He always asked the right questions so that the children told him what they had to do. He invariably gave them a choice of answers. It was never open-ended.

The choirmaster said to the singers, "When you are singing well, should your jaw be relaxed or stiff? When you are breathing well, should your shoulders go up or should they stay down?" The student noticed that the choirmaster focused their thinking by providing a clear choice.

Try it wrong!

The student also noticed that sometimes the choirmaster asked the children to do something incorrectly to enable them to experience for themselves that it was indeed wrong, rather than just take his word for it.

"Try raising your shoulders very high when you take a breath," the choirmaster said. "Are they stiff or relaxed? Are they comfortable or uncomfortable? Now try it with relaxed shoulders. Which is the better way?"

Do it right!

"The children are really teaching themselves how to do it right," thought the student. "All he's doing is guiding them along the way. What patience he has. He's also giving them a singing lesson at the same time as he's teaching them how to begin to sight-sing. He's packing a whole lot into the practice, but he's doing only one thing at a time. He makes sure that they fully understand one step before he goes on to the next. It's marvelous."

The student saw that the choirmaster was demonstrating, over and over, his five wheels.

Five Wheels in practice

1. *Be enthusiastic and the children will catch the enthusiasm or passion.*
2. *Teach in a small group so each child has your complete attention at all times.*
3. *Teach one simple step at a time and then combine it with the next step.*
4. *Marry theory and practice in everything you do. Every note the children sing, they can see.*

Every note they see, they sing. The written notes come alive for the children. They mean something to them!

5. *Be in full control. The children really enjoy singing because they can see that they are making progress all the time. This is the best kind of discipline. The children are doing it because they want to, and there's no wish to play around.*

13

Step 2
Singing the Great Scale

The choirmaster spoke to the girls, "Now, because you're doing so very well, we'll go on to the next step."

"Aha," thought the student, "Step 2." He watched as the choirmaster gradually added to the notes written on the chalkboard. First, he asked the singers if they knew what this note was. He wrote an A to the left of the G already there.

There was silence. Neither of the girls played an instrument, so all this was new to them. To help them, he showed them the notes on the piano keyboard. He introduced the girls to alphabetical naming of notes and how they were written on the staff's alternate lines and spaces. When he was finally given the right answer, he played A again and asked them to sing it as he pointed to the written note on the board.

"Now," he said, "here's G again," and he played it. "Sing it for me." He pointed to the note G. "Now sing me this note," he said as he pointed to A, but did not play it for them.

There was a slight pause and one of the girls sang A correctly. "Now this note," said the choirmaster pointing to G, barely restraining his excitement. "And this," as he pointed back to A. He then pointed to G twice and the girls sang it twice.

"Do you realize what you have just done?" he beamed. "You are reading music!" The girls looked at each other in amazement for they hadn't realized that reading music was so simple.

"Yes, you are reading music. Did I play the note A that you sang for me? No, I played G, but you were able to sing G and A whenever I pointed to them and in any order. That's reading music, and you did it!"

The student was thrilled as well and watched as the choirmaster added other notes— B, C and D—one at a time using a similar question and answer technique. "The singers tell him what the notes are because he asks the right questions," thought the student. "They're getting quicker at it. They really understand what he taught them."

The student saw that the choirmaster was still mixing theory and practice. No sooner was a note named than they sang it, sometimes without him playing it. The theory became real to the girls, noted the student. "He's integrated singing techniques with sight-singing techniques."

The student watched as the choirmaster asked the girls if they were standing well when they were singing a B. One of the girls wasn't and she hastily improved her stance. "Well done, Kathy," said the choirmaster, encouraging her. "Let's sing that note again. What's it called?"

"B!" they answered.

"He never tells them a thing. He always asks them. What a great habit to get into." said the student to himself.

Then the choirmaster started to add notes going down from G—F, E, and D, one note at a time. The girls named each note correctly and then sang it when he pointed to it.

The children found this a little difficult at first. They had only gone up before. With the choirmaster's patience and clear understanding of what the problem was and the children's own eagerness to please him, they managed it.

The choirmaster played a chord of D major on the piano and said, "Now let's try singing a downward scale to 'Ah'—like this." He modeled what he wanted as he pointed to the notes on the chalkboard. The student noticed that he insisted that the last note of the scale was sustained for four counts, coming off on the fifth as he pointed to his thumb. The choirmaster showed each beat exactly on his fingers.

"He's not mentioned sharps," thought the student. "I'll have to ask him about that afterwards." He continued watching as the choirmaster gradually introduced higher notes— E, F, and G. After they sang each note, one at a time as before, the choirmaster had the children sing downward scales starting on those notes—E flat major, E major, F major, F sharp major, and G major. He played the first note of the scale and then the tonic chord of each before the children sang the scale. The choirmaster pointed to the notes they sang with one hand while the other hand played a very light accompaniment on the piano—a series of first inversion chords.

"How very simple," thought the student, "but he's still not mentioned accidentals, even though he's playing them."

"It's interesting to see how easily he gets the children to sing with their head voices," the student thought. "They are singing those upper notes so easily. Clearly, he expects them to do it and he keeps insisting on well-shaped mouths to take their mind off how high they are going. They have no time to be worried or tense. They're really enjoying singing those high notes."

The student also noticed that the choirmaster sometimes didn't play any accompaniment because the children were singing so well. "If he doesn't have to play the piano, he doesn't," the student thought. "I don't know many choir directors who show such restraint. I must write that down."

- ***Don't play the piano when the choir is singing unless it is necessary.***

The student thought about his own brief months as a choir director and realized that he never left his place behind the piano during rehearsal. He squirmed in his seat as he remembered how many times he had given his choir the first note. "I did it over and over again," he thought uncomfortably, "but this choirmaster gives the first note only once and then doesn't give it again for a long time—even though he often stops to ask them a question. Children really can remember notes much better than most of us realize."

He watched as the rest of the practice flew by on wings of achievement. They were very attentive and responded to the choirmaster's every wish. He saw with amazement as the choir-master took the children higher and higher until they were eventually singing two-octave downward scales from a top C!

"I don't believe it," the student thought. "I had no idea that children could sing so high so easily." He sat open-mouthed as the choirmaster asked the children to do something that enabled them to sing still higher. "This is impossible, but it's actually happening," thought the student as he sat rooted to his chair. "There are so many questions I must ask him. I can hardly wait until tomorrow comes. He won't get me out of his office until he's answered every last one of them!"

The next day, the student ran to the choirmaster's office. "I found it wholly amazing to see you lead those girls in that practice yesterday," said the student as he moved some papers from a chair so he could sit down.

"Yes," said the choirmaster, "That's one of the exciting things about working in small groups. You may try all sorts of things. The children are excited, you're excited—everyone's excited. We're all in this together. Every practice can be a voyage of discovery and you may uncover gold at any time. Yesterday we certainly did!"

"How did you learn to teach children to sing so high?" asked the student.

"I learned by watching Frauke Haasemann," replied the choir-master. "She and I were teaching a course together. I was showing some students how simple it was to teach sight-singing to children. Frauke was teaching them how easy it was to enable children to sing with clear head-tone. She was interested in what I had to say, but I was fascinated by what she demonstrated.

"I came back here afterwards where I had a girls' practice. I tried what she had demonstrated and it worked. The girls showed that they could sing incredibly high. One girl sang a three-octave downward scale starting from the A flat above top C! Even though I'd been teaching children to sing all my life, I'd never known this technique before. Frauke wrote the book, *Group Vocal Techniques,* about it. Here, let me lend you my copy."

"Thanks," said the student eagerly, as the choirmaster rummaged in his bookcase and eventually found the book. "That leads me to another question," the student said. "Why didn't you intro-duce the subject of sharps and flats yesterday when you were getting the girls to sing the downward scales of D major, E flat major, and so on?"

"I'm glad you noticed that," responded the choirmaster. "In the beginning of this method, I teach the children only the basic minimum of what they need to know and what they can grasp. All they need to realize is that when notes are written going up, they sing upwards, and when they're written going down, they sing downward. You'll also have noticed that before I asked the children to sing any scale, I played the key-chord for them."

"Yes," said the student, "this gave the children the basic key tonality. They could not have done anything else except sing C sharps and F sharps once you'd established what D major sounded like."

"What else did I do to help them move from D major tonality to E flat major tonality?" asked the choirmaster. He leaned forward in his chair and fixed the student with a steady eye.

"Oh-oh," thought the student, "I've got to get this answer right." He thought for a while and then said, "I can't remember precisely what you did, it sounded so natural, but I can remember thinking that no singing teacher I've heard ever led his singers from one key to another so easily." He looked at the choirmaster, hoping that his answer would please. It did.

"Yes," said the choirmaster with a smile. "Many singing teachers I've heard totally destroy the tonality of any scale their student is singing." He went to the piano on the other side of the room, carefully avoiding a pile of anthems on the floor. "Many teachers do this when they are giving warm-up scales." He demonstrated.

"They play the tonic chord of the new scale while the student is still singing the final note of the previous scale. The clash of tonalities is awful. I really can't understand how they can do such a thing. It shows such musical insensitivity. It also means that they are not really listening to their pupil's final note."

The student grinned. "Surely that's pitching it a bit too hard, isn't it? They're not all like that, are they?"

"Well, let's put it this way," responded the choirmaster, "have you ever heard a singing teacher do what I did yesterday when I led the children from the scale of D major to the scale of E flat major?"

The student thought for a moment and said, "No, I really can't say that I have. What did you do?"

"I played just one chord that joined, not interrupted, the two tonalities. What is that chord?"

"It's the dominant seventh of the new key," responded the student. "I just remembered."

"Well done." beamed the choirmaster. "It's so very simple. If it's simple, it's generally right." He demonstrated again.

"I also noticed that once the children found they could sing scales, you accompanied them less and less," the student observed.

"Many teachers play the piano far too much. I only accompany the children when they really need it, such as at the beginning of the learning process, or if they have pitch problems. Otherwise, I just let them get on with it without interference from me.

"Playing the piano too much is a disease from which far too many choir directors suffer. It can be an active hindrance rather than a help. Children and adults have to battle against the piano if it's played badly, or sing far too loudly in order to hear what they are singing. So many choir directors not only play too much but they play too loud.

"Oh dear, oh dear!" the choirmaster exclaimed as he thumped the top of his piano, quivering again. "When will they ever learn?"

"Perhaps you ought to tell them, by writing a book," suggested the student with a grin.

"I have!" smiled the choirmaster, relaxing again. "You see," he went on, "it's the choirmaster's job to wean his singers away from relying on the piano. They often have to sing without it on Sundays. I teach them to be self-reliant, not piano-reliant."

"Can you show me some simple accompaniments for scales?" asked the student.

"Yes, there are various ways you can do it. The easiest is to play just a series of first-inversion chords, like this."

"These chords give the children a firm, helpful, harmonic underlay that enables them to pitch tones and semitones accurately. Not all children know what a scale sounds like, so you have to help them.

"If the children can pitch well, you can try playing just an upward scale in the bass while they sing downward. This helps them achieve some independence of mind in order to sing against another melody, which is what they will have to do when they sing with other voices. Listen."

"If, on the other hand, you want a really well-harmonized accompaniment, you could try this."

"There's no end to the chord sequences you can use," he turned and looked at the student with his direct gaze. "But what does it mean if you are bothered about playing fancy chords on the piano?"

"It means that you are more interested in your accompaniments than you are in what the children are singing," answered the student confidently.

"Exactly! Unless you have an instinctive chord sense that enables your fingers to think while you are giving the whole of your attention to the children, then you are not giving them what is their due. Therefore, you can't expect them to give you their whole attention unless you do what?"

"Unless you are giving them the whole of yours." responded the student.

"Right. You can write Step 2 down now," the choirmaster said as he smiled.

Step 2
Increase the notes, one by one until you get a great scale.
Sing and name each note, one at a time.

14

Checking Steps 1 and 2

"Where precisely are we in the sight-singing process?" asked the choirmaster as he resumed his seat by the desk.

"Well, Step 1 was, 'Singing one note.' You began with middle G and worked on that. You showed the children where it was on the stave by pointing to it. Then you asked why it was called 'G.' All the time you gave them a singing lesson on stance, mouth and jaw shape, breathing, and also teaching them about pulse (four counts, off on five). That took quite a while."

"Right! But did I do all those things together?"

"No," smiled the student, "you taught them one thing at a time. You made sure that each child knew exactly what you wanted from that one thing before you went on to the next thing."

"Right again. Now, what was Step 2?"

"Step 2 was an extension of Step 1. You gradually increased the range of notes that the children sang, so that they sang a group of three descending notes, then four, then five descending notes. Before long, they sang whole scales."

"What was the one crucial thing I did while they were singing these notes?" asked the choirmaster.

"You pointed to the notes as they were sung," answered the student. "Then they could see what they were singing."

"Yes, that is so very important," said the choirmaster, thumping his desk. Several stray papers fluttered to the floor. "Most choir directors, when they are teaching sight-singing, do it in compartments—mostly rote-singing with a little sight-singing thrown in on the side. For me, sight-singing is a continuing process. It is wholly integrated into the practices. Whenever the children sing anything, they have to make an attempt to read it first. Only when they have made a real effort to work it out for themselves and gained some measure of success, do I help them with notes and rhythms—should they need it.

"By the way," he added, "it's pretty obvious that you can't possibly accompany scales with two hands and point to the notes on the chalkboard at the same time. That's why my simple one-handed accompaniments are so useful. They leave the other hand free to point to the notes.

"So, let's go on to Step 3. Let's go to where it all happens—in the practice room."

15

Step 3
Step-Wise Melodies

"Step 3 is an extension of Step 2," said the choirmaster as he sat at the grand piano in the practice room. The chalkboard was cleaned and ready. "Do you remember what I wrote on the chalkboard by the end of Step 2?"

"Yes," said the student, taking some chalk and writing on the chalkboard. "You had a succession of whole notes from G down to D—a sort of great scale."

"Yes," responded the choirmaster, turning around on his high swivel chair, "keep those notes on the chalkboard. You can have great fun with them."

"Fun?" exclaimed the student. "I thought all your practices were geared to work, not fun."

"Oh, come now," grimaced the choirmaster. "weren't those children enjoying themselves as they were working?"

"Oh, yes, they were." The student paused for a moment. "Oh, I see. The fun came out of the work. They enjoyed it because they were succeeding in everything you set them to do."

"I only wish more choir directors realized that," said the choirmaster sadly. "So many of them think that fun comes first and work must be fit in afterwards. Their work becomes a chore because it's not regarded as something to be enjoyed for its own sake. For my children, the fun grows naturally out of the work we are doing.

"If it's fun they're after," he continued, "there are many less demanding ways of getting it than spending an hour in a practice room. But there is a place where they can learn and grow into the secrets and delights of music, and that's here in this room with me.

"They find, as they learn more and become more skilled, that they enjoy it more and more. They have fun and they develop an increasing self-respect. Those qualities cannot be bought. They can only be experienced.

"And this," he said, indicating the practice room with a sweeping gesture and knocking some chalk on the floor, "is where it all happens!" He paused for a moment to recover his breath, while the student restored the chalk to its proper place.

"You feel pretty strongly about all this, don't you?" the student said.

"You know I do; otherwise I wouldn't be in this business. Now, let's get on. Where were we?"

"You were about to tell me how the children could have fun—in Step 3—with those notes written on the chalkboard."

"Oh, yes! Well, what we do now is to get the children to sing tunes while pointing to a succession of notes on the great scale we have already written down."

"How do you do that?"

"In any number of ways. For example, I might begin by playing middle G."

"And point to it on the chalkboard," interrupted the student.

"Right! Also, play the tonic chord of G major. You must always remember to do that to give them the tonality in which they will sing. Then I ask them to sing the notes that I point to. For example, I might point to G, A, G. That's about as simple as you can get, but it does involve the children in being able to pitch a note going up."

"As well as a note going down," interjected the student. "You already did that with those two girls yesterday."

"Yes, because they were so good. I felt that I could get ahead quite fast with them. They worked hard."

"And they enjoyed it." beamed the student.

"We'd make a good patter act," remarked the choirmaster

with a grin. "You are doing exactly what I expect you to do. You are . . ."

"I am giving you right answers to questions that you haven't even asked me, because . . ."

"Because I'm making the next step so clear that, to you, it's obvious," interrupted the choirmaster for a change. "If you can get the children to respond to you as quickly and enthusiastically as you are doing to me right now . . ."

"I'll have the makings of a stimulating teacher," said the student. "Right?"

"Right! Now, let's get on. Where were we again?" said the choirmaster.

"You pointed to three notes on the great scale starting with G, going up one note to A, and then returning to G."

"Yes. If you are faithful in pointing to the notes as the children sing their scales, you should have no problem with getting them to sing little melodies as you point to notes on the same great scale. But there's one important thing that you need to realize."

"What's that?" asked the student.

"You tell me," responded the choirmaster. "But let me make it easier for you to give the right answer by . . . ."

"By asking me the right question." the student said quickly.

"Yes, indeed. Have the children been singing by step or by leaps so far?"

"By step."

"Yes! Do we want to stay in the moving by step mode or do we want to launch out into singing leaps?"

"That's easy. If you are going to stay with teaching one thing at a time, you keep with step movement for the present. You are about to ask them to sing up and down, which is the one new thing they are about to learn."

"Yes, indeed. Our object here is to enable the children to pitch on their own without any help from me, one note higher, one note lower. What comes next?"

There was an appreciable pause as the student thought furiously. "If you are moving by step, you can only go up one note at a time or go down one note. There's nothing else you can do, is there?"

"How does 'Good King Wenceslas' begin?" asked the choirmaster unexpectedly.

"Oh, yes." answered the student. "Notes can go up, they can go down, or they can stay the same. How obvious!"

"Did I tell you that?"

"No, you asked me the right question instead, and I told you. I'll remember that because you've enabled me to have ownership of the answer. This is great!" the student exclaimed. "I'm learning so much here."

"Thank you. That's what I'm here for—to enable you, the children, and the adults to enjoy a really positive learning experience. But we must get on.

"I point out little melodies for the children to sing on the great scale—going up or down by step and occasionally having repeated notes. The children find this great fun because it's a challenge they can win. It's good to have a competition between the children to see who can get most notes right. They love that."

The student wrote in his notebook:

Step 3
Point out short step-wise melodies from the great scale.
Use repeated notes, too.

"There's no end to the number of little melodies you can invent," said the student going to the board. "You can begin with this sort of thing." He pointed to the notes on the great scale, going left and right as needed.

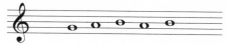

"You eventually get to something like this," said the student as he pointed to notes on the great scale.

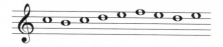

"Yes," said the choirmaster, "but you left out something of crucial importance in your second example. What was it?"

"I've no idea," answered the student.

"You were so engrossed in the simplicity of what you were doing, that you made the basic assumption that the children had not made, and could not make." He moved over to the piano, and the student stepped out of his way. "You began your first example on G, the note the children were used to starting on. They knew the tonality of the next note." The choirmaster played a G, and then he played the A above. "They expected the note above G to sound as it does because they've been singing Gs and As for several minutes. However, the second tune you asked them to sing began on a C, and what happens?"

"Oh yes," exclaimed the student, "they would still have been thinking in the tonality of G major, and so might have sung the top note as an F sharp, instead of an F natural that I had intended."

"What should you have done before asking them to sing a melody that began on a new note?" the choirmaster asked as he moved away from the piano while the student took his place.

"I should have established the new tonic by playing the tonic chord, and then the first note, like this," said the student as he played.

"I do even more than that sometimes," said the choirmaster, regaining the piano stool. "For example, if I were to ask the children to sight-sing the opening measures of the hymn "Comfort, Comfort," I would play the tonic chord and then play part of a rising and descending scale to ensure that the children hear the tonality. In this way, they sing in the right key. Listen."

Tune to be sung

Com - fort, com - fort ye my peo - ple

"Now I see," said the student. "It's so very clear."

"Of course it is!"

"Everything you do is obvious, except that I didn't think of it first."

"Right! Well, come along to the beginning boys' rehearsal tomorrow and see how obvious Step 4 is. It's completely different from Steps 1, 2, and 3. You might try to think what it is beforehand. It's something that boys particularly enjoy."

16

Step 4
Clapping Rhythms

Four boys were gathered around the piano in the practice room. For twenty minutes they were engrossed in all that the choirmaster encouraged them to do—singing one note, singing scales, improving their breathing technique, checking their stance and the shape of their mouths, working on head tone, and trying to sing step-wise melodies as he pointed to them on the great scale written on the chalkboard.

Some of the boys were more successful than others. One boy managed to sing correctly only five notes of a step-wise melody while another boy sang twenty. However, the student noticed that the choirmaster showed that he was equally pleased with all the boys. He made it plain that what he expected was equal effort, not equal results, and the boys realized this, too. They all felt good about the situation.

"Well, now then," said the choirmaster to the boys as he vigorously erased the great scale from the board, "we're going to do something entirely different."

"Here comes Step 4," thought the student. "I wonder what it is?"

"There are two ingredients for making music," the choirmaster said as he looked directly at each boy to make sure they were all listening. "One of them is pitch. What's the other?"

Several hands shot into the air. "Yes, Luke?"

"Rhythm!"

"Well done, Luke. Who else knew that it was rhythm?" Two hands shot up. "Good! Have you heard of rhythm, Chris?" he asked the boy whose hand hadn't been raised.

"Yes," said Chris.

"Can you spell 'rhythm' for us, Chris?" asked the choirmaster.

Chris made several attempts, but didn't quite succeed. "You're nearly right, Chris. Who can get it absolutely right? Yes, Brian?" The choirmaster wrote the word on the board in big capital letters as Brian spelled it out for him. "Well done, Brian."

"That's Wheel 4," thought the student. "The children are seeing what they are saying. That man doesn't miss a trick."

"Well, now then," said the choirmaster as he wrote four quarter notes on the board, "who can tell me what these notes are? Are they half notes or quarter notes?"

"He did two things there," thought the student. "First, he asked them a question as he was writing on the board to keep their attention. Second, he asked the question in the 'is it this or is it that' format, so that their thinking would be focussed. He saves a lot of time like that. If I had asked the open-ended question, 'What sort of notes are these?' I might have been given the answer, 'Messy ones!'"

"Quarter notes," said Matt.

"Quite right, Matt," said the choirmaster standing up. "They sound like this." He clapped four times, very rhythmically.

"Now, you do it with me," said the choirmaster, and the boys followed along.

The student noted that the boys clapped very vigorously in imitation of the choirmaster. It was done with purpose and energy.

"Good! Now we'll do it again as I point to these quarter notes on the chalkboard." The choirmaster pointed and the boys clapped, following the firm rhythmic pointing of his index finger. He pointed in such a way that the boys had to clap rhythmically, energetically, and together as the choirmaster's finger stabbed at the notes drawn on the chalkboard. "Good! Let's do it one more time." And they did.

"Now," said the choirmaster as he wrote a half note on the

chalkboard to the right of the four quarter notes, "what sort of note is this? Is it a half note or a whole note?"

"It's a half note," answered Brian.

"Yes, it is. How many quarter notes are there in a half note, Chris?"

There was a slight pause, then Chris said, "Two!"

"Well done, Chris. You clap a half note like this," he gave a vigorous clap followed by an equally vigorous second beat with his hands still clasped.

"Now you try it." he told the boys. There was a loud clap. "Nearly, Chris. Let's have a really strong second beat.

"That's better. Now," he added, as he drew a second half note next to the first, "let's clap both half notes as I point to them."

The student noticed that the choirmaster pointed to the two-beat notes with two very clear movements of his hand. It was quite clear that those notes had two beats by the way he pointed to them. The choirmaster firmly pointed at the top of the note for the first beat, and then he slid his finger down to the bottom of the stem with a rhythmic jerk for the second beat. "He made it very obvious; anyone could follow that," thought the student.

"Now, let's clap these four quarter notes and the two half notes." The boys did exactly that, as the choirmaster continued to point at the notes very rhythmically so there was no possibility of anyone making a mistake.

"Were we absolutely together?" he asked after they finished. The boys shook their heads. "Okay, let's do it again and keep absolutely, absolutely together." And they did. They saw that the choirmaster had set a high standard for what he regarded as right. He knew they could do it if they really tried; and they knew it, too.

"Finally," said the choirmaster as he drew a whole note on the board after the second half note, "what is this note?"

"A whole note!" they said together.

"Yes! How many quarter notes are there in a whole note?"

"Four!" they all shouted.

"Okay, who can clap me a whole note? Yes, Brian, you do it."

Brian clapped and clasping his hands, moved his forearms vigorously for the count of two, three, and four.

"Well done, Brian! Let's all clap the whole note as I point to it." And they did.

"Now, let's clap the whole thing." said the choirmaster pointing to the four quarter notes, two half notes, and one whole note.
And they did.

"Was that absolutely together?"

"No," said the boys.

"Shall we do it again?"

"Yes!" they chimed; so they did.

"Now, let's have some fun," said the choirmaster, getting busy
with eraser and chalk as he altered the notes. "Who can clap this
for me?"

 Four hands shot into the
air. "All right, let's take it in
turn. You're first, Chris."

Chris clapped as the choirmaster pointed to the new set of
notes. There was one mistake.

"He'll show Chris which note was wrong and get him to do it
again," thought the student to himself.

"That was pretty good, but was it all correct, Chris?"

"No," said Chris.

"Whoops," thought the student, "I forgot. He'll ask the lad
where he went wrong. When will I ever learn?"

"Where did you go wrong?" the choirmaster asked Chris.

"On the last half note. I clapped two quarters instead."

"That's right. Do it again." Chris did and was right.

"Good. Let's all do it." And they did.

"He's involving them all as much as he can, while giving individuals the opportunity to try it on their own," the student thought.
The pace was quick, continuous, and totally absorbing. There was
nowhere else in the whole world for these boys. They were totally
present in body, mind, and spirit. "That's real concentration for
you!"

The choirmaster gave each boy a fresh rhythm to clap on his
own, followed immediately by everyone clapping the same example. As the time came for the practice to finish, the director gave
the boys a really long example to clap. "Let's finish with everyone
clapping this absolutely together—right the first time!"

The boys clapped as the choirmaster pointed rhythmically to
every note. It was a great effort.

"Was that absolutely together?"

"No," the boys responded. They clapped it again.

"He didn't have to ask them to clap it again," observed the student. "They knew he wouldn't be satisfied until it was right; and they want it to be absolutely right themselves. He just raised an eyebrow as much as to say, 'Let's go!' and they did it again."

On the second try, it still wasn't together. The choirmaster didn't say a word, but gave them an encouraging look. He raised his eyebrow once more, and off they went yet again. This time it was absolutely right.

The boys all stood, glowing with pride and pleasure at having achieved so much. The student could see that the choirmaster fully shared their feelings of accomplishment. He could see that they were all in this together. The choirmaster was part of their team and they were part of his.

The student recognized that the choirmaster really knew how to teach children so that they wanted to learn. It was fun because it was hard work first and there was a clearly defined goal. "The achievement was its own reward. What a practice!" thought the student. He wrote Step 4 in his notebook:

Step 4
Clap simple rhythms exactly right.

17

Getting It Exactly Right

The following week the student was again in the choirmaster's untidy office. He noticed that a chair had been cleared for him to sit on. "An improvement." he thought.

"Well," said the choirmaster, "what is Step 5? It's a logical step from Step 4."

The student cleared his throat and said, "Do you teach the children how to clap rests and dotted notes?"

"That could be," answered the choirmaster enigmatically. "There's no hard and fast rule about what one should teach next. For example, if you felt strongly that children should learn the Kodaly method, or Solfege, or whatever, you could certainly make use of these admirable techniques. What is the main difference, then, between my method of teaching children to sight-sing and all other methods?" the choirmaster asked unexpectedly.

"You insist on everything being right?" ventured the student.

"That's very important. Many choir directors are satisfied with things being nearly right. Once their children get it into their heads that being nearly right is acceptable, then that is the standard the choir director will get for everything. The notes of anthems will be nearly right. The singers will arrive for practices and services nearly on time. They will nearly put the choir first in their order of priorities.

"There's only one way to go, and that is to get everything

wholly right. From this, everything else flows—the anthems are sung wholly right, practices start and finish punctually, and respect for the choir is high.

"Do you know," he added, "one boy came to me last week, he's a fine tennis player at school, and he said, 'Choir comes before tennis!' I was thrilled. But he wouldn't have said it if all I expected from him was 'nearly.'"

"Is that the main difference between what you do and what some other choir directors do who teach sight-singing?" asked the student.

"It certainly is a difference, but not the main difference. Let me ask you the right question. How much time do I spend teaching sight-singing here?"

"Oh, you spend the whole time. You said that every part of your practice is geared to sight-singing. The children have to work out everything for themselves. You don't tell them a thing," responded the student.

"Yes, that's the main difference. We practice hymns and anthems like any other choir. We aim at beautiful tone and singing well together—just like everyone else. But the singers know that they have to do the thinking. I will not do it for them. They come ready to work. What is the end result of all that?"

"Their skills are improved at every practice by the work they do. They go home feeling that they have spent that hour really well."

"Yes! The term is, I think, 'rosy glows.' I aim at sending every singer home with a rosy glow, and absolutely exhausted because of the effort he or she made. That way they'll be back for more next week. But let's get back to Step 5," said the choirmaster.

18

Step 5
Clapping from Music

The choirmaster looked carefully at the student and said, "If Step 5 is an extension of Step 4, what is Step 5?"

"Well," said the student, "if it's not teaching them about dotted notes, I can't think what it is."

"Let me ask you the right question. From where have the singers been reading music so far?"

"From the chalkboard in the choir room."

"Right! But from where will they be reading music for the rest of their lives?"

"From printed anthems and song books." There was a pause. "You start them singing songs from hymnals and anthems!"

"Very nearly. You are right when you say that they must start singing from the printed page. Are there many differences between singing from the chalkboard and from the printed page?" the choirmaster asked casually.

"Not really. The writing is bigger on the chalkboard, but otherwise it's pretty much the same."

"Oh, do you think so?" said the choirmaster quietly. "What color are quarter notes on the chalkboard?"

"White. They're black on the printed page. I hadn't thought of that."

"Right!! What else hadn't you thought of?"

"Half notes change from black to white. There are bar-lines. Alto parts that get in the way—stems up and stems down. There are words," continued the student, warming to his task, "and expression marks. Yes, I can see that singing from the printed page is very different from singing from the chalkboard."

"You've left out several other major differences," said the choirmaster. "For example, when we've been singing little melodies from the board that move up and down by step, in which direction did we point?"

"You had to point right and left on the great scale. On the printed page the music always moves to the right."

"You mentioned that words are a new factor. So are extra staves for tenor and bass, which the young singer has to ignore. Singers have to find out where to go when the end of a line comes. Do they go down one line or two? In most hymnals the trebles have to skip a line."

Text: William Kethe, d. 1608?
Music: *Old 100th,* Melody from *Pseaumes Octante Trois de David,* 1551, alt. harm. after Louis Bourgeois, 1510?–1561?

"For accompanied choir music, the sopranos not only have to skip the men's line, but also the organ part. That's another thing to be learned. Of course," added the choirmaster, "when everyone has a book, I can no longer point to the music for them to follow, so we have to do something else!

"Let me tell you what I do. Telling you isn't a good method of teaching, but time is short and we need to get on. I get children to share books. One child follows the notes with his or her finger, while the other child does the singing, then they exchange roles. I walk round to each pair to check that the right notes are being pointed to at the right time. This takes a lot of careful supervision. The children are not wholly secure in doing this yet. After a little while, I can spot which child is doing it particularly well and which child needs more help. What do you think I do to help those who need it most?"

"You put the better child with the less experienced," replied the student.

"Yes. Children love to show off their knowledge in front of their peers. If you can organize this in a non-threatening and constructive way, you will ensure that the less experienced child will try even harder to match the skill shown by the other."

"I would imagine that the more experienced child will also improve."

"Yes, indeed. That's a very perceptive comment. Do you remember what the best method of learning is?"

"It is to teach!" blurted out the student.

"I certainly learned more when I began to teach than I ever did when I was a student. It's the same for most people, I believe. If you can cast some of your children into the role of teachers, they will improve as much, or even more, than those whom they are teaching."

"So what exactly do you do for Step 5?" asked the student.

"I make it as accessible as possible for them," answered the choirmaster. "On the chalkboard, I write out several measures of rhythm from a hymn tune and get the children to clap it."

"Do you use quarter notes, halves, and whole notes only?" asked the student.

"Yes, of course. This is not the time to introduce anything new."

"Then I ask them to clap that same rhythm from the hymnal without telling them that it is the same rhythm."

"There is always someone who realizes that it's the same. I get them to clap it again—both from the board and the hymnal—and then they all realize it. Then I ask them to tell me the differences between the way the two rhythms are written out, the differences which we discussed a couple of minutes ago. Why do I ask them to tell me, rather than vice versa?"

"Because everything they tell you they will remember, but anything you tell them they can forget. You asked me that question before," the student added with a grin. "That's why I remembered it."

"Well done." laughed the choirmaster. "You have the makings of a creative teacher. You remember things. You notice things and you have a good sense of humor. Having a sense of humor is essential, not only to help make life more pleasant for the children and yourself but also to save your sanity when things go wrong."

"Do things go wrong for you?" asked the student.

"Good heavens, yes! Nearly every day there's some problem to deal with. That's what life is all about. It's how you deal with those problems that makes or breaks you. Being able to laugh at yourself is a marvelous safety-valve.

"While we're at it, there's another essential quality that choir-masters must possess if they are to fulfill their vocation and retain their sanity, and that is stamina."

"What do you mean by that?" asked the student.

"A choirmaster must have an abundant reserve of physical and mental energy. Choirmaster must always appear before the choir radiating goodwill—even when they've had a bad day. They must spread enthusiasm—even when they are not feeling their usual fer-vor. They must disseminate inspiration—even when they think they are in the wrong business! Choirmasters must 'keep on keeping on' in the face of every setback. That's what they are there for—to lead from the front at all times." The choirmaster paused to take a breath.

"To lead a live program," he continued, "such as we have here that involves so many people of all ages, means that the choirmaster must expect to meet with many problems, as well as to reap many rewards. That's why stamina is vital. Not too many students realize this when they seek to become church musicians. But let's get back to Step 5."

"You were telling me how the children were clapping rhythms from printed music," said the student, somewhat subdued by what he had just heard.

"Yes! That is a most important part of learning to read music. The children must acquire the skill to follow the notes precisely— to look at the right note at the right time. I sometimes find that when a child has a problem in reading a piece of music, the problem disappears as soon as I go over to him or her and point out the notes myself. I don't have to say anything. I just help focus his or her attention exactly where it should be."

"In other words," observed the student, "the child wasn't looking at the notes really closely. He or she was looking in the general area of the notes and so was making mistakes."

"Right again. You need to stay with Step 5 for a fair amount of time. However, this does lead us directly to Step 6."

But before he continued, the student wrote:

Step 5
Clap simple rhythms from printed music.

19

Step 6
Melody and Clapping

"Now can you tell me what Step 6 is, if I tell you that it is very closely linked with Step 5 with one of the wheels added to it?" the choirmaster asked the student.

"Oh dear," thought the student "this could be a problem." He gathered his courage and said, "I know it's not having a passion for it; that's already happening. You always work in small groups, so it's not Wheel 2. You're still teaching one thing at a time and you're in full control, so it's not Wheel 3 or 5, so it must be Wheel 4—'See and sing, sing and see, marrying theory and practice.' But I can't think what it is," he ended helplessly.

"You've done well to narrow it down to the correct wheel," said the choirmaster. "Just think for a moment. Here we have children clapping rhythms of simple tunes, but what's that got to do with music?"

"Oh, yes!" exclaimed the student, smiling again. "There's no tune coming into the situation at all!"

"Right! They're just clapping and it seems to bear but little relation to music. What I do, once they are able to clap rhythms without too much help from me, is to get them to clap the rhythm of a tune while I play the melody with them on the piano. They suddenly realize that what they're clapping has a close relation with music. It turns the theory of clapping into the practice of music. It comes alive for them in a new way."

"Let me write that down," said the student.

Step 6
Play the melody as the children clap rhythms from the printed page.

"How do you play the tunes for them?" asked the student. "Do you play them with their full harmony underneath or do you play just the melody line?"

"You can answer that yourself." said the choirmaster.

"You only play the melody line because the harmony could confuse them, couldn't it? Especially if it had cross rhythms," responded the student.

"I often play the tune in sub-octaves for them, because it makes it easier to hear when they're making such a noise with their clapping."

"That's very simple, isn't it?" observed the student. "But you had to challenge me to think before I got there."

"That's okay. I spend much of my life doing that. That's the only really effective way to teach, as you now know. But I wish that many more teachers and choir directors knew that. We'd have much finer choirs if they did. Come back tomorrow and we'll finish the whole process. We're nearly there."

"I thought you said there were twelve steps to learn how to sight-sing. We've only reached Step 6," wondered the student.

"Don't worry, the remaining steps can be accomplished very quickly with just one exception. I'll reveal the final steps to you tomorrow."

20

Summary of Steps 1–6

The next afternoon found the choirmaster and the student sitting in the choirmaster's office once more. Two chairs had been cleared of papers and the pile of anthems that had been in the middle of the floor was now stacked outside the door.

"My word," observed the student, "your office is getting neater."

"I wouldn't go so far as to say that, but it is less of a mess. Once I've finished these sessions with you, I should be able to get on with some of the paperwork that's been piling up during the last few weeks."

"I'm sorry if I've been a cause for your problems," responded the student, rather uncertain of himself.

"I didn't mean for you to take it like that," said the choirmaster easily. "We all have to do what we have to do, and you are my top priority at the moment. I've chosen to tell you as much as I can, in as short a time as I can, about the gentle art of teaching sight-singing. Your education is, for me, top of the list. You're enjoying it and I'm enjoying it, so let's get on with it.

"Run through for me, very briefly, the first six steps of the sight-singing process."

The student picked up his notebook and began to turn the pages.

"No, no!" said the choirmaster hastily. "If you have to look them up in a book, you don't really know them. They need to become so much a part of your instinctive thinking that you will reel them off from memory. What is much more important, however, is that you will put them into practice when you have your own children's choirs to teach. It has to be all up here," he said, tapping his forehead, "ready to come out at a moment's notice."

"Okay," said the student, closing his book and looking straight at the choirmaster, trying to imitate his direct look when something important had to be said. "Here they are:

"Step 1: Singing one note in rhythm and see the written note.

"Step 2: Sing downward scales and follow the notes with your finger.

"Step 3: Sing simple step-wise melodies from the great scale.

"Step 4: Clap simple rhythms written on the board.

"Step 5: Clap the same rhythms from the printed page.

"Step 6: Same again, but have the tunes played at the same time.

"And always teach one thing at a time." The student smiled to himself.

"Well done!" said the choirmaster predictably. "Now let's go to the practice room and charge ahead with the remaining six steps."

21

Step 7
Singing Pitch from
the Hymnal

The student and the choirmaster walked into the sunny practice room together. The choirmaster sat on his high swivel seat behind the grand piano while the student stood to one side, his notebook and pencil ready.

"Step 7 is an extension of Step 3—singing step-wise melodies pointed out on the great scale," said the choirmaster. "Let's write out the great scale now." Quickly and neatly, the choirmaster wrote the notes from top G through to middle D on the chalkboard.

"Why don't you go right down to middle C?" asked the student. "So much music is written around that note."

"So much bad music is written around that note!" corrected the choirmaster. "I am appalled that so many choir directors inflict immature, so-called music on their children's choirs that is not only devoid of musical inspiration with inadequate theology, but which also gives the children no opportunity to sing with their God-given head voices!"

"I see you feel strongly about that," observed the student.

"I feel passionately about that!" corrected the choirmaster

again. "Don't start me on that subject or we'll be here all day. Being a child in a choir is all about singing with the head voice—singing top Gs as easily as middle Gs. Very few children's choirs are allowed to do this because of the deluge of rubbish that is published for them. All of it is pitched too low and their choir directors seem to have no idea how easy it is to enable children to sing with their head voices.

"Recently a choir director flew over 1,000 miles to spend three days here watching me lead my children's practices. On the third day she told me that she hadn't realized that children could sing real music. She had heard my children sing compositions by Handel, Gibbons, Byrd, Duruflé, Howells, and many others. Would that other choirmasters realized this, too.

"Although I do teach the children about middle C, I don't really use it with the younger children. It's a different matter with the older children—the fifth through eighth graders—who have a full two-octave range or more. They can sing both with their head voices and their chest voices. But let's get back to Step 7—singing melodies by step," said the choirmaster.

"I first get the children to sing a simple melody from the hymnal by pointing to the appropriate notes of the great scale written on the chalkboard."

"Don't you use any special sight-singing books?" asked the student.

"Yes. The 'special sight-singing book,' as you call it, is the hymnal. It's the book the children use every time they come to a practice and it's full of first-rate material that is ready and waiting to be used to enable kids to read music.

"I know what you are really asking me, and the answer is no; I don't waste money or time on buying so-called sight-singing exercises. Everything you could possibly need is right here," he said, picking up a hymnal and waving it vigorously, "if choirmasters would only take the trouble to look.

"I've been through the whole hymnal and picked out melodies that move by step, melodies that introduce simple rhythms and more complex ones, melodies that introduce accidentals, and so on.

"The whole bedrock of my teaching system here is that nothing gets in between the singer and the music in the singer's hands.

My aim, which is a successful aim, is to give a song to a singer and say 'Sing it!,' and they do!" The choirmaster got up and walked around the piano slapping it as he went.

"Wow," thought the student, "there's a whole lot of passion there."

"So," said the choirmaster as he subsided on his swivel seat again, "for the third time, let's get back to Step 7.

"I choose a tune from the hymnal that moves by step and I point out the first line on the chalkboard like this—it begins on G."

"But you first play the tonic chord and the first note," interjected the student.

"Well done. Yes! Here we go." The choirmaster pointed to the first eight notes of "Old Hundredth" using the great scale (G, G, F, E, D, G, A, B).

"This could be the opportunity to introduce some practical teaching about accidentals, if you have the time and the inclination, because F sharp appears in this melody," commented the choirmaster. "That's up to you. If the children can't see the keyboard, you could leave it alone. But if a child asks a question about the F sharp, you must answer it then and there; and that takes time, if you are going to do it properly."

"Do you get the children to sing the melody in the correct rhythm?" asked the student.

"That's a good question. You give me the right answer."

"The answer is no. You would be asking the singers to do more than one thing at a time. They're just concentrating on pitch, not rhythm," replied the student.

"Well done. But you did right to ask the question so you know exactly what you're aiming for. You could, if you wished, write out the melody from the hymnal on the chalkboard," continued the choirmaster. "This could be an easy intermediate step to enable them to translate the notation they've seen on the chalkboard to the notation they will see in the hymnal. That's up to you. Eventually, you must ask them to sing that same melody from the hymnal."

"Do they have to sing the whole hymn tune or only part of it?" asked the student.

"Only part of it. Here it will be the first eight notes. If the children can sing eight notes right, they can eventually sing eighty notes right. But you need to get to the printed page as quickly as possible. Why is that?"

"Because that's what they'll be using from now on," said the student with a smile.

"Right! When you transfer the children's attention to the printed page, what must you be very careful to do? There are several things."

"Well, the first thing you must do is to play the tonic chord, and perhaps play a scale up and down, to establish the tonality of the music, like this." The student leaned over the choirmaster's shoulder and played.

"Well done, again. You needn't play the whole scale. A few notes up and down are all that is needed. It would be helpful, too, if the children would sing those few notes with you, just to get the 'vocabulary' of the notes into their heads before they attempt to work out the melody for themselves. Treat it is a warm-up exercise to get their mouths into the right shape. So many children sing with almost closed mouths when they are working something out.

"Always make the answer accessible to them, but leave enough for them to work out on their own so that they can own their right answers. Challenge them, but don't make it so difficult that they are threatened. Once the children get it into their heads that reading music is not difficult, then you will be well on your way to success," commented the choirmaster.

Without being prompted, the student added, "And the second thing to do, is to ensure that the children are looking at the right notes at the right time. You may have to point to the notes yourself as they sing them from the book, or else ask a more advanced chorister to stand with them."

"Good," said the choirmaster. "Remember that it is your object to make the children as independent as quickly as possible. They need, very soon in the process, to practice following the notes with their own fingers, supervised by you, of course.

"One of the surprising things I discovered when I began teaching children how to read music was that they often have a problem in distinguishing between notes written on lines from those written in spaces." The choirmaster drew a G and an A on the stave.

"You mean that children can't immediately spot the difference between a G and an A?" asked the student.

"Yes. They often mistake a G for an A. You have to point clearly to the two notes and get them to look more closely at them. Do I tell them if the second note is different from the first?" asked the choirmaster unexpectedly.

"No," responded the student immediately, "you ask them."

The choirmaster continued, "You might say, 'Is this note higher or lower that note?' You may have to ask the question several times before a child really sees that the notes are different and gives you the right answer."

"I suppose it's similar to a Westerner being asked to distinguish between Chinese or Japanese written characters," observed the student. "They all look much the same until you study them closely."

"My word," exclaimed the choirmaster admiringly, "that's a very intelligent comparison. I must remember that. By the way," he added, "some children aren't aware that it's the position of the note head that determines the pitch, not the stem. Until you explain this to them, they might think that A with its stem up is higher than B with its stem down. This is because, at first glance, it does look higher.

"When I had just graduated from college," he continued, "I was given one of the most important pieces of advice I'd ever heard. It came from Dr. Gerald H. Knight, the distinguished director at the Royal School of Music in England. He said, 'When you give a child a piece of music to sing, he looks at the words and not at the notes.' I didn't believe him at the time, but I've since found this to be true, many times."

The choirmaster got up and began to wander around the practice room, waving his arms to illustrate his point, "One of your tasks is to discover devices that will assist children to look at the right notes and to follow them closely.

"There are a number of ways to help focus the children's

attention on the notes when you are playing melodies for them. Here are some examples.

"Ask them to put up their hand when you reach the last note in a line of music. They won't be clapping here, of course, just following the notes with their fingers.

"Ask them to put up their hand when you play the note G or any other specified note.

"When they are a little more advanced and they can sing the melodies, ask them to sing a note to the word 'up' when a note goes up, 'down' when it goes down and 'same' when it is repeated. The first note, by the way, is always 'start'.

"This is great fun. The children love it. It's fun for adults, too. So, for example, the first phrase of 'Good King Wenceslas' would be: start, same, same, up, down, same, down. The children have to supply the words, of course, you don't write them out. That really makes them think.

"It's a great device to help children learn new music at the early stage of your introducing a sight-reading program to your choir. You don't need to use it when their reading is really established. But at this early stage you can play the melody through with them several times as you use the ideas I've just given you," continued the choirmaster. "They hear it several times, but throughout this process, the children are thinking, they are not just being fed mindlessly with notes, as so many of them are, alas."

He began thumping the top of the piano again to show how opposed he was to choir directors who teach their children by rote. "All these devices help to focus the children's attention on the right note at the right time and thus, they will be learning a little better at each attempt how to read music."

"That's fascinating," said the student. "I'd love to try that when I get my own choir. It's all very simple, but it works. I've heard your big choirs singing and every singer knows exactly what he or she is doing. They are all trained musicians. But where are we in Step 7?" asked the student. "We've been talking about so many other things as well."

"Yes," agreed the choirmaster. "Although I try to put things in nice neat boxes, there are always a host of other things that need to be said. Step 7 in a nutshell goes like this.

"1. Get the children to sing a step-wise melody to 'Ah', or some other tone-producing vowel, while you point out the tune to them from the great scale. That's the same as Step 3.

"2. Get them to sing the same melody from the printed page in the hymnal; it need only be a few measures. Thus, the children are introduced to singing from the printed page.

"3. Remember to take no notice of rhythm at this stage. Just get the pitch right, so take it slowly."

"You must always preface the children's singing by playing the tonic chord and a few notes of the scale, up and down," added the student.

"Well done, indeed! That sums up the essence of Step 7. Now let's race along through the remaining steps."

"Let me write down Step 7 first," said the student.

Step 7
Singing pitch from the hymnal — no rhythm yet

22

Step 8
Pitch and Rhythm from
the Hymnal

The choirmaster said to the student, "Step 8 is a simple extension of Step 7. What do you think it is?"

"Well," said the student, comfortable in his productive relationship with the choirmaster that enabled him to take his time when thinking out loud, "the children are singing from the printed page by now. They are singing the pitch of notes accurately. So it seems to me that they now need to be able to sing those same notes in rhythm."

"Hole in one!" exclaimed the choirmaster. "But would you expect the children, once they'd sung the pitches correctly, to add the rhythm to those notes immediately?"

"I expect some of the brighter children could," mused the student, "but it might be wiser to approach the joining together of pitch and rhythm a little more cautiously."

"Right again! If you do have a bright bunch of children, by all means let them have a go at singing the melody in pitch and rhythm straight away. Children must always be permitted to go at their own pace. That is true if their pace is fast, as well as if their pace is slow. Let the bright children leap ahead. This will show the other children what they will be able to do. Never hold children back; it discourages them. The bright ones need to be encouraged as much as the less gifted."

"What do you do with the children who outgrow your learning classes?" asked the student.

"Once they've learned what they needed to know in that particular class, I promote them to the next grade up where they can be with slightly older and more experienced children. But that's a subject we must deal with when I show you just how simple it is to train a choir if you know the great secret!"

"I thought we'd already discussed the great secret," said the student."

"Yes," interrupted the choirmaster. "That was one of the two great secrets. The second great secret is even more important. I only wish I'd known it when I first became a choirmaster, but I had to wait for many years until I discovered it. We'll go into all that very thoroughly at another time. We will talk about everything else you've ever wanted to know about how to train a really first rate choir and have your choir stalls overflowing with enthusiastic singers."

"You ought to write a book in which you reveal with all these other secrets."

"I have, don't you remember?"

"Oh, right." replied the student.

"Let's stick to the sight-singing right now," said the choirmaster. His eyes twinkled at the prospect of revealing still more gems to this student who was so obviously destined for great things.

"I can hardly wait," exclaimed the student as he walked round the piano, banging on the lid in his excitement.

"Let's finish Step 8," said the choirmaster. "There isn't room for both of us to go charging around this room like a couple of windmills that are out of control!"

"Sorry," said the student, relaxing once more with his elbows on the closed lid of the grand piano.

"Never apologize for being enthusiastic. There's too little of it around as it is. You can only communicate with your children if you are enthusiastic and really believe in what you want to teach them."

"Have a passion for it," interjected the student.

"Yes, indeed! We were discussing how to introduce rhythm into the singing of the pitch of the melody the children had just worked out. Or rather, into the singing of part of a melody," said the choirmaster correcting himself. "You need only deal with two or three measures at a time. If a child can sight read two measures correctly, he or she has the potential to sight read the whole of *Messiah*. But you needn't do all that in one practice just to prove your point."

"Agreed," said the student. "How do you introduce the matter of rhythm once the pitch is correct?"

"Well, I just go back to Step 4."

"Clapping rhythm," interjected the student.

"Yes, clapping rhythm. Once the child has sung the two or three measures in correct pitch for me, I then ask him or her to clap the rhythm of the same few measures Once the child realizes that there are two separate and distinct ingredients to this process, we can then begin to put pitch and rhythm together."

"Do you find that children do this easily?"

"It varies," said the director. "Some get it right straight away, but others need leading very gently, sometimes note by note, before they really get it. Help them get the first note right, then the first two, then the first three, and so on. It's like learning to ride a bicycle," he continued. "Some children can steer a fairly straight course down the road almost at once, but others seem to find themselves always going into the nearest thorn bush. You just have to be sensitive. By the way, which one of the five wheels do you need to keep in front of your eyes?"

The student thought for a moment and said, "Get one thing right at a time."

"Yes, indeed. If the child cannot get the first note in rhythm, then there's no point in going on to the second note. So this is where it is particularly important to work with small groups of children, for each one will need your individual attention at this point in the learning process.

"I often find that children like to be given a couple of chances to get something right before you go on to the next child in the group to see if he or she can get it right. Once you've established friendly rivalry between well-matched children in a small group, their will to win is whetted and they try even harder to get it right."

"What do you do with a child who doesn't seem to be able to keep up?" asked the student.

"Your question shows a quick sensitivity that marks you out as a caring teacher," observed the choirmaster. The student glowed, but tried not to show it.

"The child who can't keep up with the rest of the children should be given an individual, immediate goal to fulfill in front of his or her peers that can be achieved. For example, if the other children are working at getting two measures correct in both pitch and rhythm, the other child might be asked to sing just the first note correctly. You could say, 'Bill, I want you to sing the first note to 'Ah' for two beats and show us all just what a splendid mouth shape you have!' When he does it, you say to the other children, 'Now I want you to sing the first two measures with mouths as beautifully shaped as Bill's.'

"And then," continued the choirmaster, "once the other children have that little melody right, you say, 'And now we'll finish by all of us singing it together.' Bill joins in with the rest of them and, more often than not, he finds himself singing it correctly. How did this happen, when he couldn't do it right before?"

"I have no idea," said the student. "Could it be because he has listened to the others and learned from them?"

"There's a lot of truth in that," answered the choirmaster. "By the way," he continued, "when the children are singing on their own, what must you ensure?"

"You must ensure that the other children are fully occupied."

"Yes, you must insist that they follow the notes with their fingers in their own copies of the music while another child is singing on his or her own. Children will turn off at the slightest excuse. They are like adults in that respect, so this calls for constant vigilance on your part."

Quickly, the student responded, "That's why you like working in small groups. You can keep your eyes on everybody to ensure that they are all doing what you expect them to do."

"Yes, it's a constant battle, but if you tell the children very clearly what is expected of them, they will tend to respond to you if you really show that you mean what you say. If you let them begin to get away with inattention, having told them that you expect attention, they'll immediately sense that you don't really mean what you say. They will push your boundary as far as they can. Once you're in that position, you're on a very slippery slope. Always mean what you say and follow it through!

"It's much kinder to the children when you are consistent in this way. Choir directors who say one thing, but let their children get away with unhelpful behavior, are being grossly unfair to the children. The children have no idea where they stand. Children respect firmness, as do adults, and that's the only way you can hope to build up a fine choir.

"Discipline means not only well-ordered behavior, but its root meaning is 'learning'. The twelve disciples of Jesus were learners. Your choir children and your adults should all be disciples and you must lead from the front everywhere you wish them to go." The choirmaster paused and wiped his brow after this speech.

There was a silence. The student was very impressed by what he had just heard. Nobody had told him about these matters before and he knew he wanted to learn much more about this vital, practical subject. Perhaps it would be in the choirmaster's book.

The student spoke, "You haven't told me why Bill was able to sing the melody correctly when the other children were singing with him, but he couldn't manage it by himself."

"This is one of the great deceptions in choir training many choir directors fall for, I fear," said the choirmaster seriously. "Children are great imitators. You would be amazed at how quickly children can follow a tune played on the piano. They can sing each note so quickly after you've played it that you believe they are reading the tune. Instead, they are really following what you play.

"Young Bill was not singing with the children, he was singing after them. He did it so quickly that he and the others didn't realize it. Alas, more often than not, the choir director doesn't realize it either."

"That's why you can teach sight-singing effectively only in small groups," observed the student. "You need only one or two children in a choir who can sight-sing and everyone else follows them and the choir director doesn't realize it."

"Yes, indeed! The choir director becomes fooled that all the children can read music, whereas it's only a very few, perhaps those learning an instrument, who are doing all the work. Leaders are wonderful people, and we all need them. Part of our task here is to train singers to lead. Once you have a couple of strong leaders, you've got yourself a choir. But when those leaders are absent, you realize that the choir isn't as good as you thought it was.

"This is where working in small groups can be such a marvelous help. In small groups you are training people to think for themselves, not just to follow mindlessly what others are doing. Not too many choir directors do that, I fear," the choirmaster added sadly.

"Now that I've been watching you at work and talking with you," said the student, "I should be more aware of some of the pitfalls to avoid and know which straight paths I should follow."

"If that weren't true. I would have been wasting my time," said the choirmaster, raising his eyebrows to his receding hairline. "But I don't think I've been wasting my time. How do I know that?"

"Because I've been responding to you all through," answered the student quickly. "You haven't just sat me down and talked at me, you've talked with me and required from me a response to everything you've said."

"That's how all children's practices should be run," said the choirmaster, "but how few of them are." He paused for a moment and then went on. "We're nearly done. Let's get on to Step 9."

"Not before I've written down Step 8." said the student as he opened his notebook.

Step 8
Sing pitch and rhythm from the hymnal

23

Step 9
Speaking Words
in Rhythm

"There's one ingredient we have not yet introduced into this matter of singing hymns and songs," said the choirmaster as he turned on his swivel stool and began to clean the chalkboard. "What is it?"

The student thought for a moment and said, "The children are singing the pitch and the rhythm correctly by now. It could be that they need to pay attention to expression. No, that's possibly more advanced. Oh, I know," he said, slapping his knee rather hard. "They haven't yet dealt with the words!"

"Right yet again! This is something entirely new and it needs to be integrated gently, firmly, and very clearly into the situation."

"How do you do that?" asked the student, rubbing his sore knee.

"You do it by combining it with Step 4."

"Clapping rhythm," interjected the student confidently.

"Clapping rhythm, indeed! You get the children to clap the rhythm of an easy hymn tune. Only a few measures are needed. Don't attempt the whole tune unless they are very bright. They'll be good at this by now and should be able to do it right, first time.

"Then you ask them to read the words, normally. Have them read just the words under the first few measures. Then ask them if they can clap the rhythm while they speak the words in rhythm."

"That's pretty easy, isn't it?"

"Surprisingly, it's not. A number of children experience real problems when you put clapping and speaking together. It's like rubbing your tummy with one hand while you pat your head with the other. They can get really tied up in knots. So you need to proceed slowly and with a lot of care."

"How do you do that?" asked the student.

"Let me list just three ways for you," said the choirmaster.

"1. You can get the children to read the words in rhythm while you clap yourself.

"2. You can divide the group in half, one half reads while the other claps, then change over.

"3. If you have a small group where there's a happy spirit of cooperation, you can ask one child to speak the words in rhythm while the others clap. Continue round so that each child has a turn. Once one child has it right, all the children will be able to do it."

"Because children can imitate so quickly." the student said confidently.

"Yes, but let them enjoy their triumph with that particular phrase and then go on to another one. We aren't in the business of having children copy what others do but to help them think for themselves and come up with a solution to their musical problems."

"I imagine that once children have the idea of speaking words in rhythm, it gets easier and easier for them," the student added.

"Yes, it does. But you also have to realize just what children are being asked to do when you set them this challenge. How many things are they looking at when they speak words in rhythm?"

"Obviously, they are reading the line of words," began the student.

"Yes, and be aware that words printed under a melody often look very different from words printed in a book. Why is that?"

The student thought for a moment and said, "When you have a song with a number of stanzas, the words are printed in rows with the first stanza at the top, the second underneath, and so on. The children must be able to find the right line to go to when they reach the end of the first line."

"Yes, and as you sing the second and third stanzas, the words get progressively further away from the notes. That can make singing a new song very tricky.

"That's the second thing about reading a song," continued the choirmaster. "The children have to look at two lines at once— words and music. Unless you are very firm, they will look at the words only and not the notes."

"I hadn't realized how many different things we are asking children to do when we put a new song in front of them." said the student.

"That's not all," continued the choirmaster. "You haven't told me why the words themselves look different on a music page as opposed to a storybook page."

"The words under music are hy-phen-a-ted," enunciated the student very clearly. "That changes their appearance drastically. I imagine that some children would have a real problem with that."

"They do indeed. Even with simple words like 'sing-ing,' 'peo-ple' or 'foun-da-tion.' Also, in many churches, children have to tackle Elizabethan English, which is a whole different problem. Ask a child what 'trespass' means and she'll tell you every time that it means 'you mustn't go onto other people's property;' and of course, she's right."

"But all these problems can be handled if you tackle just one thing at a time." laughed the student.

"You've got it! Let's go on to Step 10."

"Not before I've written down Step 9." said the student, getting busy with his pencil.

Step 9
Speaking words in rhythm

24

Step 10
Putting It Together

"Well now, what is there left to do?" asked the choirmaster.

The student eagerly responded, "Let me see. The children are singing the notes in pitch and rhythm. They are speaking the words in rhythm. The next step must be putting all three elements together so they can sing the words in pitch and rhythm."

"Yes," answered the choirmaster. "You ask them to put together the three separate and distinct ingredients that go to make up a song. You ask them to attempt just one or two measures at a time so that they are more likely to succeed rather than fail. Set them a goal they can achieve, rather than one which they cannot."

"That's Wheel 3," observed the student. "Teach one simple step at a time."

"Yes. You can spend a lot of constructive time working on two or three measures of a song; but do you remember what else we've been doing while we've been teaching them to sight sing?"

"You integrate everything else that a singer needs to know, such as breathing, stance, vocal production, and so on. You don't teach sight-singing in a vacuum, you give them the whole package, one thing at a time."

"Right! Once the children have reached this step of combining words, pitch, and rhythm, you've achieved what you set out to do. They are reading music for themselves. It doesn't matter that the music is simple. Once they can tackle simple music successfully, with continual practice, they will be able to sing increasingly complicated music."

"Let me write down Step 10," said the student.

Step 10
Combine pitch, rhythm, and words.

"I thought you said that there were twelve steps to this matter of learning how to read music," observed the student. "It seems to me that you've reached your goal in ten steps. The children are reading music right now!"

"That's true. But you've only come along so far. I gave you a hint a minute ago about what Step 11 might be. It's a big step. What do you think it is?"

25

Step 11
Everything Else

The student thought furiously about what could have been omitted from the teaching method the choirmaster had presented so clearly. "I mentioned that singing with expression should be taught at some time," volunteered the student.

"True. What note values haven't we touched on yet?"

"Oh, lots of them. Eighth notes, dotted notes, rests, and, of course, we haven't really mentioned sharps and flats . . . ."

"And naturals," interrupted the choirmaster, "and slurs and ties and repeat marks and time signatures and bar-lines, on and on. So what do you think Step 11 is?" he asked with a mischievous grin.

"Well, I suppose Step 11 is teaching everything else!"

"You've got it! This is the step that takes more time than anything else because there is virtually no end to the techniques that you can teach. But you will find that if you've taught the basic techniques thoroughly, the more advanced matters will come more easily."

The student quickly wrote:

Step 11
Teaching everything else!

Teaching dotted notes

The choirmaster continued, "Do not tell the children that a dot adds one beat to a note, because it clearly doesn't—except for half notes. You may have to do some unlearning here. Many children are poorly taught about dotted notes in school and elsewhere.

"Show them, very clearly, with lots of written examples on the board, that a dot makes a note longer by an extra half of its length. This is a concept that young children will find difficult to grasp at first. Have them tell you why a dotted half note is worth three beats and why a dotted whole note is worth six beats.

"I often continue after that by saying, 'Suppose you could dot a number 8, how many beats would it be worth? Suppose you could dot a number 10,' and so on. I also show them what a dotted Jill looks like: Jill plus half-of-Jill, or what Jill will look like in a few years' time.

"Give them plenty of clapping exercises with dotted half and whole notes, and they really will get the idea."

"Dotted quarter notes could be more difficult," observed the student.

Teaching eighth notes

"Yes, you are right. Before you can touch dotted quarter notes, you have to enable the children to clap eighth notes. This part is easy. Ask them the right question: 'How many eighths in a quarter?' If they aren't sure, show them what an orange looks like when cut in half, in quarters, and in eighths. You don't need a real orange, you can draw it on the chalkboard. Use visual teaching as much as possible so as to get the message home.

"Once they have grasped the concept of eighths as being half the size of quarters and therefore they go twice as fast, you can start incorporating pairs of eighths into your rhythmic clapping, like this."

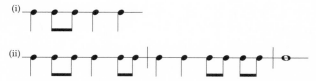

"It's also fun to divide your singers into groups with one section clapping continuous quarters, then another section clapping halves at the same time, and a third section clapping eighths, and so on. Move the note values around from group to group. That really makes the children concentrate and they learn a great deal from this practical exercise. You might also like to introduce 'time names' (Ta-aa, and so forth) which many children learn at school. These can be helpful.

"Of course, you will have found lots of examples of real music in the hymnal or song book that have pairs of eighths them, so that they can clap and sing those. Beware of inventing lots of wonderful exercises that could take you away from your main source of music, the hymnal and simple anthems.

"At this point, when they really know what eighths feel like, you can introduce the concept of dotted quarters."

Teaching ties and bar lines

The choirmaster continued, "In order to help children understand ties, you must help them clap a number of rhythmic passages with ties in them, like this."

"What else will you do about ties?" asked the choirmaster.

"I'll look for examples of ties in the hymnal or the song book and show them how they work, especially in relation to the underlay of words," answered the student. "By this time they'll need to understand the concept of bar lines and time signatures."

"Yes, they will. You see why Step 11 will take so much time. So many of these new concepts are interlinked.

"But now they're ready to understand all about dotted quarters. Get them to clap this."

"Then get them to clap the same passage, but with two ties added, like this."

"Show them that they can feel the beat of the first tied eighth note in each group with a vigorous arm movement."

"Ask them to explain how that rhythmic passage could be rewritten using dotted notes. They may need a little help in this, but they need to see that these two passages are identical."

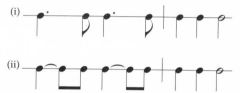

"Ask them to clap both so they can really experience that they are the same. Then show them that to clap dotted quarters, they need to feel the dot, as they felt the first tied eighth. All this will take time and much patience on your part, and you may have to repeat your instruction the next time you see them. But once they've got it, they've got it."

Accidentals

"How do you teach accidentals?" asked the student.

"Ah, yes. Accidentals," said the choirmaster smiling. "I almost forgot about them. Teaching accidentals needs the use of the keyboard to show the singers how an accidental affects a note. Show them the rise or fall of a half step and then get them to sing them. Mix theory and practice as you have been doing for all your other teaching and the message will come through clearly."

Rests

"In many schools the clapping of rests is done by showing a 'hands apart' stance (like saying, 'I don't know'). I don't think much of this. It doesn't give the rest any feeling of rhythm.

"What I do, and what the boys and girls love, is to get them to mark a one-beat rest by digging themselves in the ribs with both elbows—hard, like imitating the flapping of wings of a duck.

"I also encourage them to grunt when they do this. It makes a rest a real experience, so that this passage would sound like this."

clap   clap   clap **grunt**   clap   clap   clap **grunt**   clap **grunt** clap **grunt**   clap 2 3 4

"Wouldn't the grunting get in the way when the time comes for them to clap real music?" asked the student.

"Yes, of course it would. But, because you have the children on your side through your constructive relationship that has been developing over the weeks, you can get them to turn off the grunts when necessary. Allow them to do it once, with grunts for the fun of it, and then to do the dig-in-the-ribs silently."

Teaching intervals—The Third

"The first interval you can teach is that of the third. In England, there's a bird called the cuckoo that sings a falling minor third. Children can quickly grasp this and can learn to pitch falling minor thirds from any note. You need to remember to give them the first note and the tonality. If you

Cuck-oo

were to ask them to sing a falling minor third from B, you wouldn't play the chord of E minor for them, but either E major or G sharp minor. Thus, the note they have to find is already somewhere in the chord they've been given.

"From this step you can then move to the hymnal and find examples of falling minor thirds. Explain to the children that thirds go from space to adjoining space, or line to adjoining line. Show them on the keyboard why they are called thirds. Some children think of them as the fraction one-third, which is entirely mistaken.

"Now the interesting thing is that the children can also pitch major thirds in the same way. If you give them B again and ask for a major third, you'll get it if you play the chord of G major to establish the tonality.

"Having got this far, you need to tackle rising thirds. Clearly if 'cuck-oo' is a falling third, then a rising third must be 'oo-cuck'."

The student laughed. That was a good one! But he could see that it would work, if the concept were introduced patiently, one step at a time with plenty of visual aids and practical examples.

The choirmaster continued, "The children can spot them very easily in hymn tunes that you will have selected—where there are 'cuck-oos' and where there are 'oo-cucks.' Get them to sing the tunes to 'la' but to change to the bird call, 'cuck-oo' or 'oo-cuck,' when necessary. Here, try singing this section."

La La La La La La La La oo - cuck La La La cuck-oo La La

Other intervals

"If you have come this far, you will find that children are able to begin to pitch other intervals fairly accurately, especially if you play the harmonic basis of the song with them as they sing. But what will you not do?"

"You won't play the melody with them," answered the student.

"Why not?"

"Because the children, being quick imitators, will follow what you play a fraction of a second after you've played it, and so they won't be exercising their sight-singing technique. They won't be thinking, they'll be following."

"Yes, and how many choir directors do you think play the tune for their singers?"

"About 99 percent, I should think," said the student with a grin.

"I'm afraid you're right. That's why most children in choirs can't sight-sing. The choir director is doing all the work for them. You know that singers will let their choir directors work as hard as possible; it's a subliminal game with them—'If he wants to work that hard, let him.' You've watched me long enough, what is my game?"

"To make the singers work as hard as possible so that they will improve every time they're with you." responded the student quickly.

"Yes, indeed! But let's get back to the teaching of intervals.

"I encourage my singers to look at the notes they are singing and also at the notes they have sung. Frequently, you'll find in music that a tune leaps to a note that the singer has already sung. If the singer can be trained to look out for these moments, then the singing of intervals becomes much easier. The example that comes readily to mind is that familiar hymn tune, 'Old Hundredth,' that begins like this."

"Young children have no problem at all in pitching the sixth note because they've already sung it twice. Once you begin teaching the singing of intervals like this, you'll find that the singers can quickly grasp it, and they begin to make all sorts of connections with other notes. For example, the next phrase in 'Old Hundredth' has another leap of a fourth that goes to a note they've not yet sung."

"Get them to tell you that the C is one note higher that the two Bs they've just sung. Get them to sing B and C in sequence several times, then they will be able to sing that phrase correctly. From this basic skill they will gradually build up greater skills as time goes on. But, again I remind you, don't play the melody with them, or all your work in teaching them to sight read will go for nothing."

"Show me the sort of accompaniment you would play," said the student

"Here's what I would play for those first two phrases of 'Old Hundredth.'"

"Is that all you would give them?" asked the student incredulously.

"Certainly. The melody moves by step, except for the two leaps that we've already dealt with. All you need is a clear bass line to give the harmonic structure of the melody. You'll have noticed three other things about the bass. First, I keep the quarter note pulse going on longer notes. Second, I'm playing detached so that the singers can hear themselves easily. What is the third thing?"

"You play softly." said the student.

"Yes! If you take nothing else away with you from these sessions we've had together, at least take with you how to play the piano for practices. In a nutshell it is, play hardly at all and play *piano!*" They both laughed.

26

Step 12
Over and Over

"That's about it, I think," said the choirmaster as he got up from his swivel stool and led the way out of the practice room.

"What about Step 12?" asked the student, hurrying after him. "You haven't told me about that."

"Oh, you can work that out for yourself as you have all the other steps," said the choirmaster as he turned out the lights and prepared to lock the door. "I'll give you a hint. If a singer has sung a middle G quarter note correctly once, does that ensure that he or she will always sing that note correctly?"

"No, of course not," answered the student.

"No, indeed. We all make mistakes. We all forget some of what we have learned and we need to be reminded again and again. So what is Step 12?"

"Step 12 is doing everything we've learned over and over again—whenever we need to or when we've forgotten what we thought we knew," said the student laughing.

"Quite right," said the choirmaster as he walked towards his car. "You can use any one of the eleven steps at any time you need them. For example, if you are learning a particularly difficult anthem, you might get the children to clap the rhythm while you play the melody. That's Step 6. Remember?" said the choirmaster.

"You can use the great scale for warm-up exercises. Point to the notes you want them to sing on a sustained vowel. Divide the singers into two groups and have one half sing the notes you point to with one hand, while the other half sings the notes you point to with the other. That's great fun. It's like playing a living organ! Just keep these steps before you when you are leading practices, and you'll know which to use at any one moment. They're all geared to success. I know they work, you know they work, and..."

"The children know they work," both men said in chorus. They were of one mind.

27

First Ending

"I must be going. Can I give you a lift back to college?" asked the choirmaster.

"Thank you," said the student, as he tried to get into the choirmaster's car that was almost as untidy as his office. Papers littered the back seat and there was a box of music on the passenger seat the student had to move before he could sit down. "There are two questions I've been wanting to ask you ever since I came here, but the opportunity never seemed right."

"What are they?" asked the choirmaster as he steered his car into the stream of evening traffic.

"Well, the first has to do with the tidiness of the practice room," ventured the student.

"And the untidiness of my office," laughed the choirmaster. "It's simple, really. It's all to do with priorities. Some people are born to be tidy and others, like me, untidy. But the important thing is that this job gets top priority because it affects so many people.

"We have 120 singers in our choirs, some churches have even more than that, as you know. Take them and the members of their families together, many of whom have close ties to the church, and you come up with a list of 300 or more people. These singers spend from one to six or more hours a week in my practice room. My first priority, therefore, is to ensure that they know they are coming into a well-ordered situation where they will feel comfortable and welcome. That's why the practice room is kept tidy and efficient. There's a pastoral and a spiritual side to this job we haven't mentioned. Neatness is an outward and visible sign that we care about them, and I think they know it.

"As to my office and this car, well, I can only do so much, and it is I who have to live with it. I've promised myself that I'll reform, one day." He laughed as he drove the car ever nearer to the college. "What's your other question?"

"Well, it's to do with the choir that I had before I came here. I couldn't control the children. They gave me a really bad time. There was one girl in particular whom I had to speak to every few minutes. She was misbehaving, sitting down when others were standing, or not singing when she should have been. Yet, when the time came for me to leave, she gave me a thank-you card she'd drawn herself. I was amazed. From the way she behaved, I thought she didn't want to have anything to do with me."

"My dear young man," said the choirmaster as they approached the college gates, "don't you realize that she was 'naughty' just because she did like you? The surest way to get your attention was to be a bit of a pain. She knew that that was a sure-fire way of getting you to talk to her. That's the basic reason why children are a problem in class. They want the teacher's attention and they know how to get it—by being a pain. Once children understand that to follow the choir director's way really is in their own interest, you will have created a firm bond of trust between you and all sorts of wonderful things can happen.

"There's a lot I've picked up over a long life about all sorts of things, and keeping order in class is just one of them."

"Is that in your book?" asked the student as the car slowed down near his dorm.

"It certainly is, and many other things as well. Here we are. I'll see you on Sunday."

"Thank you, and good night," said the student, as he turned to walk to his room. He knew he had a lot to think about. It had been a great experience to see such a live program in action. "I'd love to lead a choir program like that," he thought. "Perhaps I will one day."

28

Second Ending:
A Dream

The student didn't sleep much that night, for he had been so stimulated by everything he'd seen and heard during the last few eventful weeks. He found himself dreaming that he was leading a choir of one hundred children in the practice room. They were standing around the piano with their eyes shining as he encouraged them to sing downward scales ever higher and higher.

Their mouths were open "deep" (jaws down, tongues flat, and lips coming forward). Their breathing was well controlled, their tone was like that of angels on a good day. Whenever he asked a question, one hundred hands shot into the air from children who were eager to give him the correct answer.

"Right, girls and boys," he said in his dream. "Let's look at this chorus from Handel's *Messiah*. Has anyone sung this before?"

"No!" shouted the children in happy and expectant unison.

"Okay, then we'll read it right now!"

The children eagerly found their places and showed that they were ready by standing proudly, looking at him expectantly again.

"Wow," thought the student, "don't they look good!" He began to play the introduction to the chorus, "All We Like Sheep." He played it at a steady pace, for he knew that there were some running sixteenth notes coming on the second page. "The children must be able to do what I ask them to do," he thought. "I shall challenge them, but only within their capability of being able to rise to the challenge successfully."

The children began to sing. "They're doing it right!" thought the student. "It's right, it's wonderfully and beautifully right! They are reading music so well, so intelligently and so creatively. And they're enjoying every moment!"

As the children continued to sing, in his dream they merged into a full choir of one thousand voices singing in Carnegie Hall before a packed audience as he conducted them, accompanied by a symphony orchestra.

"This is what life is all about," he thought as he waved his baton ever more musically. "This is what I'm here for; this is the greatest privilege and joy that I can ever imagine. I've trained these singers so that they are leading themselves and leading this audience to the very gate of heaven itself through the great power of music. Hallelujah!"

The student suddenly woke up and realized it had all been a dream. "No, by golly," he said as he sprang out of bed in the early morning light, "I'll make that dream come true. That's what I'm going to aim for; that's what I'm going to do the rest of my life.

"I'm going to enable children to fulfill their highest potential in music—one step at a time. I will give them a gift that will illuminate them for the rest of their lives. I shall train children not only to sing great music beautifully but also to be able to read it at sight!

"Some of them will be so inspired by what they find they can do under my direction, that they will become choirmasters and pass on the skills they've learned to the next generation. And so it will go on and on—an endless procession of trained musicians, brought up to worship God and to enjoy him for ever, through the ministry of music. Wow and Hallelujah!"

To the readers

You can be part of this, so don't just sit there. Get up and begin trying these simple techniques one at a time with your own choir, for they really work!

Your own dreams can become a living reality, and your achievements will become an ever-increasing joy to you and to all who benefit from your talent and enthusiasm. So, get up and go!

29

Teaching Adults to Sight-Sing

The student spent the next ten days on a concert tour with the college choral society. Even though he relished singing in such a fine choir whose performances were enjoyed by large and appreciative audiences, he missed his contact with the choirmaster and wondered what was going on at the church.

The evening after he returned, when the day's lectures were over, he rushed to the church music building and ran up the stairs two at a time. Outside the choirmaster's office he had to steer his way round four large trash bags that were full of papers. "What's been going on here?" he thought as he knocked on the choirmaster's door.

"Come in," said the familiar cheery voice. The student opened the door and stood transfixed. The office was immaculate. There wasn't a stray piece of paper in sight. The chairs were empty, the floor had been vacuumed, and the choirmaster was sitting at his desk on which was a small pile of letters he was answering.

"Welcome back, young man," said the choirmaster as he stood up to shake the student's hand. "How did the tour go? We've missed you."

"I've missed you, too," said the student still trying to take in the unaccustomed neatness that greeted him. "What's been happening here?"

"Well, as you were away, I felt that this was the time to do something about my office," said the choirmaster with a smile. He resumed his seat and waved the student to one of the other chairs.

"How nice to have a choice of chairs to sit on," thought the student.

"Last week I was talking with one of our choir parents who is a company executive," continued the choirmaster. "He told me that he always gets to his office two hours before the secretaries arrive so that he can clear his paperwork before the phones start ringing. He said it's the only way he can stay ahead.

"I've been following his example for the last three mornings and found that it really works. Not only have I answered all the mail that's been collecting dust for the last few months, I've also cleared out all my old files. There must be at least a tree's worth of paper in those trash bags out there. I feel like a new man!" He grinned broadly.

"When you stop learning in this life," he added, "that's the time to give up. Now what can I do for you this evening?"

"All our talks about teaching sight-singing were focussed on children," answered the student. "When I conducted a church choir before coming here, I found that most of my adults, as well as the children, couldn't read music. How would you teach them? I suppose it's much the same as teaching children, isn't it?"

"Yes and no," responded the choirmaster, as he turned to face the student.

"Good," thought the student, "I'm in for another learning experience. I must stay on my toes."

"First, you can't treat adults like children, that's pretty obvious. The fun-and-games strategy we use with small groups of children that helps along the learning process is not appropriate for grownups. Your relationship is no longer that of parent to child, but it's a curious mixture of teacher to pupil, while maintaining a good-humored and courteous adult to adult rapport. Of course, very few adults would be able to spare the time to have weekly lessons in sight-singing, although you may find some who could.

"The yes part of my answer has to do with what you teach. The no part is how you teach it."

"What do you mean by that?" asked the student as he took his well-worn notebook from his pocket.

"Let's take for granted that you lead choir practices for adults in a way which always encourages them to think, rather than expect you to do their thinking for them."

"And not many choir directors do that!" interrupted the student with a smile.

"Yes, indeed," said the choirmaster as he gave the student his direct look. "Tell me some specific things you would do to encourage your adults to think."

"Here we go, back to the thinking mode again," thought the student. "I really wanted an easy ride this evening, but with this man I never get it." Out loud he said, "There are a number of things I'd do to encourage them to think. Let me list them for you and you tell me how I did.

"1. Announce the music you want to rehearse once only to encourage them to listen to you.

"2. Once they have found their place, ask them to sing the first note, without playing it for them. This makes them look at the music creatively.

"3. Then give them the note and the first chord and get them to start singing—playing a light accompaniment.

"4. When a problem in pitch or rhythm crops up, let them try to solve it first rather than have you do it for them."

"Well done!" beamed the choirmaster. "Make sure, when a problem does arise, that you get it defined very closely, possibly by asking them what went wrong. For example, you might say: Was that rhythm wholly accurate? Which note was wrong? Was it too long or too short? When you have the right answer, show them how they can correct it by saying: If you sing the final consonant of *God* on the fifth beat, you'll find that that note will be exactly four beats long instead of the three-and-a-half you sang before.

"If you follow that pattern for rehearsals, incorporating a little basic teaching of skills each week and getting them to follow through, you will find your adults' sight-singing ability will improve.

"By the way," he asked, "from where will you conduct some of the practice?"

"Not from the keyboard, but walking around in front of the choir so that they won't rely on the piano. They'll learn how to become self-reliant rather than piano-reliant," the student responded.

"Well done!" said the choirmaster again. "What's more, when you are standing close to your singers, you'll be able to hear individuals more easily. The better you know your singers' capabilities, the more helpful you can be to them.

"That's the yes part of my answer. Always lead your rehearsals in such a way that every singer will have to think, and so that they will go home having learned at least one new thing—both in theory and in practice. This works as well for adults as it does for children.

"The no part of my answer is how you give individual or small-group teaching. I find that from time to time, adults are willing to come to the choir room for Saturday morning workshops. Do I invite all the choir to come or just some?" he asked unexpectedly.

"Oh, just a few," said the student looking up from writing in his notebook. "You can get more done with a few than with many."

"Yes. Learning to read music is a technique that can best be acquired by individuals working in small groups. Each person must be able to visualize the pitch or the rhythm. It's all too easy to follow the singers next to you if they are better than you. And because you will have to ask individuals to sing during these sessions, they must feel secure about failing in front of their peers. This is more difficult for an adult than it is for a child, and so the smaller the group the more at ease they will feel."

The choirmaster continued, "I restrict the number of adults who attend to not more than six per workshop. By doing that, you find that others want to get in on the act. Therefore, you can create a waiting list for the next workshop which is always a healthy sign.

"During practices, you can quickly spot those singers who need help most," added the choir director. "Do you know how?"

"I suppose they have a sort of blank look on their faces when singing music that is new to them," guessed the student.

"They can, indeed!" said the choirmaster. He stood up and walked around his orderly office to stretch his legs. "This is turning into a long session," he mused. "They'll also stand out by the way they turn their pages," he added as he resumed his seat.

"How do you mean?" asked the student.

"What is an essential technique you must acquire if you are to read music well?"

"You must hold your copy of the music so that you can see the conductor as well as the music," said the student hesitantly.

"Yes," said the choirmaster slightly testily, for he was not getting the answer he was looking for. "All singers should do that. But excellent sight-singers do something that others don't." There was a silence. "Are the good sight-singers looking at the same notes as the less skilled singers?"

"Yes, because they're all singing the same music," answered the student somewhat desperately, for he was aware that he was clearly missing the point.

"No, they're not!" said the choirmaster, banging his desk with his fist. "The bad sight-singers are looking at the note they are actually singing, or even worse, the note they have just sung. The good sight-singers are . . ."

"Are looking ahead to the notes they're about to sing!" interrupted the student with a great sense of relief. He'd just realized what the choirmaster was driving at.

"At last!" said the choirmaster with a sympathetic smile. "That took rather a long time, didn't it?"

"Yes," responded the student, shifting his position in his chair. "It's the same with chess players," he added hastily, trying to regain some of the points he'd just lost. "The losers tend to think only about their next move, whereas the winners think about the move after next, or even further ahead."

"That's an illuminating analogy, young man," said the choirmaster encouragingly, for he realized that he'd given the student an uncomfortable few minutes and he needed to redress the balance. "The further ahead you look when reading music, the better you tend to be.

"By the way," added the choirmaster, "I said that you can quickly spot singers who are having problems with their sight-singing. Do you think many choir directors have this ability?"

"Perhaps not," responded the student uncertain of himself. He didn't want to give a wrong answer that might invoke the choirmaster's ire again.

"I phrased the question unfairly," said the choirmaster with a comforting smile. "All choir directors have the ability to spot how their singers are doing, but very few of them actually look at their choristers while they are conducting or playing. Many choir directors have their heads firmly buried in their copy of the music and have no idea what problems their singers are experiencing.

"You, young man, will need to practice looking at your choir at least for the first couple of measures when you conduct the beginning of an anthem and at least twice for every line of music thereafter. You only make creative contact with your singers when you look at them.

"I must admit," he continued, "that I used to think that I was looking at my singers until a friend took some photos of me during a choir practice. I found that in every picture I was looking at my music instead of at my singers. That really shook me. I wish that more choir directors were really aware just how much time they spend looking at notes they know so well—or should know so well—and how little time they spend on eye contact with their singers." He slapped the top of his desk several times to express his frustration.

"While we are at it, there's another thing. Far too many choir directors get cross with their singers when they sing wrong notes. Why is that unhelpful?" he asked.

"Because the choir director isn't enabling the singers to discover why they are wrong," answered the student confidently.

"Right you are! Singers don't sing wrong notes on purpose, but simply because they don't know how to sing the right ones. The choir director who's head is stuck in her copy will not be able to put her finger on the problem that leads singers to sing wrong notes. She won't realize what they are thinking. Conducting has more to do with the expression on the conductor's face than it has to do with what she does with her hands. Similarly, the expression on singers' faces will speak louder than the notes they are singing—if the conductor is looking at them.

"To get back to my original question," he resumed, "how can you spot the less experienced sight-singers?"

"They are the ones who turn the page after everyone else." said the student with a smile. "I remember some of my singers doing that in my last choir. It used to drive me crazy. They were never ready for what was coming next."

"You'll be able to do something about that when you have your next choir to train, won't you?"

"Yes, if you tell me what you do during your Saturday morning workshops for inexperienced sight-singers," said the student trying to emulate his teacher's rather challenging manner. "If he can do it to me, I'll do it to him," he thought.

"Okay," responded the choirmaster with haste, "this is what works for me.

"1. Set a date and time for your workshop well in advance and tell your choir what you propose. A two-hour session in the early morning is good for your first workshop. That will enable adults to have most of the day still available for other activities.

"2. A month beforehand, tell them again and put a sign-up sheet on the bulletin board with only six spaces for names. Leave room for extra names for singers who would like to come if someone drops out.

"3. The week before, remind those who have signed up both by an announcement at choir practice and by sending them a reminder card. With the best will in the world, there's always someone who forgets.

"4. On the day itself have coffee and cookies ready. You'll all need a break after an hour.

"5. Have ready sets of simple music that you can use to teach the clapping of rhythm and the pitching of notes. You'll also need your chalkboard for a lot of visual teaching.

"6. Run through in your mind the basic steps of teaching sight singing we discussed during the last few weeks so that you'll be able to use any one of them at a moment's notice. You should be able to spot what problem a singer is dealing with, whether it's being unable to visualize the pitch of the next note, or some question of rhythm or whatever. Your experience in teaching children will prove invaluable here.

"7. Write down a possible schedule for your two hours, such as the following ten-minute segments:
- Welcome and coffee.

- Explaining the function of G and F clefs. Show how the staves are related as two parts of one eleven-line stave, with the middle C-line erased, to make for easier comprehension. By the way, have them stand around your piano, rather than sit in a formal row. That will make communication easier. You should have some chairs handy, for they'll want to sit down at some time.
- Naming and singing basic notes (such as G, and notes on spaces in treble stave; F, and space-notes in the bass stave.)
- Naming and singing a full range of notes on both staves.
- Singing individual melodies that move by step, pointed out on the chalkboard, as in Step 3 when teaching children.
- Break
- Introducing rhythm and clapping of notes.
- Introducing function of bar-lines, time signatures, and expression marks.
- Beginning to sing melodies and clapping rhythms from the hymnal.
- Beginning to sing music of a simple anthem.
- Rehearsing part of an up-coming anthem with special emphasis on sight-singing with the singers doing all the thinking by your asking the right questions.
- Answering their questions.

"8. When you begin, be prepared to abandon all your carefully thought-out plans for the morning," the choirmaster concluded, raising his eyebrows.

There was silence for a minute as the student hastily completed his notes. "Why did you say abandon your teaching plans?" he asked. "Your schedule seems so obviously appropriate."

"It is a good plan," answered the choirmaster, "but you would be surprised at how many misapprehensions adults have about the reading of music. They've lived for twenty or more years without knowing the basics of music, and so they've accumulated a whole lot of baggage that has been built on misconceptions and half truths. You may find, as I did, that your first session will be spent in clearing away a jungle of musical garbage.

"You'll discover where they are within the first few minutes, for they'll begin to ask questions that will show you what issues should be addressed. Like every good teacher, you need to have a lot of information and know-how at your finger-tips. A period spent in training children to read music is invaluable when preparing yourself for the more difficult task of training adults."

"Why is it more difficult?" asked the student.

"Because adults are more set in their ways. They find it harder to take new ideas on board. Their brains are not as receptive as those of children. But what you will find," added the choirmaster as he stood up again, clearly indicating that the session was nearly over, "is that adults will express their appreciation to you more readily than children, not only for what they have learned from you but also for your courtesy to them in giving them time on your otherwise free morning. You will all feel good at the end of the workshop and they'll ask for another one. Once you begin to offer your adults such practical encouragement, you'll find not only that their sight-singing will improve wonderfully but something even more significant will occur."

The student knew better than to ask what it was, for he knew the choirmaster would be sure to throw the question straight back at him. Instead, he thought for a moment and said, "I suppose their commitment and involvement with everything you are doing will be strengthened."

"It will indeed, young man," exclaimed the choirmaster turning to give him a beaming smile as they reached the bottom of the stairs. "The choir is a second home for so many of our adults. Here they find welcome, encouragement, and security. Several of them have become quite emotional when they've opened up to me about some of their personal problems. They've told me that singing in a choir, such as we have here, is one of the most creative, significant, and supportive activities in their lives and in the lives of their children."

He led the way outside and locked the door behind them. "As choirmasters, we need to realize just what an awesome responsibility we have toward our singers—not only musically but also pastorally. We choirmasters and instrumentalists can trace our lineage through J. S. Bach to King David and beyond. What a privilege!"

"Wow!" murmured the student faintly. He was, for once, lost for words.